Prairie Nurse

Prairie Nurse

Marie Beath Badian

Prairie Nurse
first published 2017 by
Scirocco Drama
An imprint of J. Gordon Shillingford Publishing Inc.

Scirocco Drama Editor: Glenda MacFarlane
Cover design by Terry Gallagher / Doowah Design Inc.
Cover photo: Lana Carillo, Michael Torontow, Sarah Cornell.
Blyth Festival 2013. Photo by Terry Manzo.
Author photo by getting captured photography

Printed and bound in Canada on 100% post-consumer recycled paper.

We acknowledge the financial support of the Manitoba Arts Council and The Canada Council for the Arts for our publishing program.

Production inquiries should be addressed to:
mbadian@gmail.com

Library and Archives Canada Cataloguing in Publication

Badian, Marie Beath, author
Prairie nurse / Marie Beath Badian.

A play.
ISBN 978-1-927922-31-6 (softcover)

I. Title.

PS8603.A33442P73 2017 C812'.6 C2017-900710-6

J. Gordon Shillingford Publishing
P.O. Box 86, RPO Corydon Avenue, Winnipeg, MB Canada R3M 3S3

For Mom.

Marie Beath Badian

Marie Beath Badian is a Toronto-based playwright, performer, director and arts educator. Her plays include *The Making of St. Jerome* (Next Stage Theatre Festival, nominated for three Dora Mavor Moore Awards) *Mind Over Matter* (part of AutoShow, Convergence Theatre) and *Novena* (UnoFestival Victoria, Toronto Fringe Festival.) Her radio work includes *Yellow Rubber Boots* (CBC *Out Front*) and an adaption of *Novena* (CBC Radio, *The Drama of Immigration).*

Marie Beath was Playwright-in-Residence for fu-Gen Asian-Canadian Theatre Company (2008–2009) and Project: Humanity (2010–2011). She was a member of the 2010 Hothouse Playwright Unit at Cahoots Theatre Company, 2011 / 2013 Tarragon Playwright Unit, 2015 Soulpepper Playwrights Circle and the 2016 Factory Theatre's Natural Resources work creation group.

Marie Beath spent two seasons as Director of the Blyth Festival Young Company, two seasons as Co-Director of Youth Programs at Nightwood Theatre, two seasons as Associate Artistic Director / Associate Artist at Theatre Direct Canada, and five seasons as the Program Director for the Play Creation Unit at Carlos Bulosan Theatre.

Acknowledgements

The development of this play was made possible through the generous support of the Blyth Festival's Roulston Roy New Play Development Fund, and the Ontario Arts Council. The play received formative development through Theatre Passe Muraille's Buzz Festival and Cahoots Theatre Company's Hothouse Playwright Unit.

I am eternally grateful to Eric Coates for championing the seed of this story even before I knew it was a play. My sincerest gratitude goes to Peter Smith, Deb Sholdice, and the cast, creative team and crew at the Blyth Festival. A very special thank you to Sue Minr for her patience, cheerleading, and above all, friendship. Thank you to all the wonderful actors who workshopped the play during its development. *Maraming salamats* to Caroline Mangosing and Darrel Gamotin for the Tagalog translations.

Thank you to the wonderful people in Saskatchewan who shared their stories and opened their hearts and homes to my mother and me in 2007—Helen and Tim Soucey, Patricia Hackett, Marie Anne Lussier, Charlie Govenlock, Rose Welchman, and Penny Ong.

To my family and extended family—Hugo Badian-Parker, Rudy Badian, Allan Badian and Gina Cervini, Jim and Wanda Parker, Lynda and Duncan McGregor and Jesmen Mendoza—thank you for your unwavering support, wisdom and guidance. To Paul Parker, thank you for creating the Arborfield Flyers' Big Play, for being my sounding board, my sanity and my partner on this adventure of ours.

Lastly, thank you to my mom, Concepcion Saberon Badian. In 1967, you took a chance on a place called Saskatchewan. Because of you, we are here.

Playwright's Notes

This is a fictional play based on real-life folks. My mom immigrated to rural Saskatchewan from rural Philippines in 1967. She came to be a nurse in a small community hospital. She stayed in Saskatchewan two years before moving to Toronto.

In September 2007, I took my mother back to Saskatchewan—on the fortieth anniversary of her arrival in Canada. We returned to the village where she was stationed—Arborfield, Saskatchewan—a tiny farming community, population 300.

To our surprise, many of the people that knew Mom were still there—other nurses and people who lived and worked in the community. And the first thing they would say when they saw Mom was, "Where's the other one?"

Who's the other one?

Her name is Penny. She was the only other Filipino nurse assigned to Arborfield. We had not planned to see her, as my mother rarely spoke of her, except to say that Penny didn't seem to want to be there. Though both their contracts were for two years, Penny stayed just shy of a year, moving away shortly after sponsoring her fiancé's emigration from Manila.

On a whim, I typed Penny's name into the SaskTel search engine and found her in Saskatoon. On the day we were scheduled to leave Saskatchewan, we sat down with Penny in an airport café. She was short, sweet and grey-haired. And she looked very much like my mom.

From that encounter I was tickled by the idea of what it must have been like back then in 1967, when no one could tell them apart. When everybody thought they were like two peas in a pod, but in truth had nothing in common other than nursing and the Philippines.

So *Prairie Nurse* was born: a partly-true-but-mostly-fiction play about My Mom, The Other One and Everyone Else Who Couldn't Tell them Apart.

Production History

Prairie Nurse premiered at The Blyth Festival on August 9th, 2013 with the following cast and creative team:

Patsy Hackett ....Jess Abramovitch
Marie Anne Lussier ....Sarah Cornell
Puring Saberon ....Stephanie Sy
Penny Uy ....Lana Carillo
Charlie Govenlock .... Rob Torr
Wilf Klassen ....Ryan Bondy
Dr. Miles .... Michael Torontow

Directed by Sue Miner
Stage Manager—Crystal Macdonnell
Assistant Stage Manager—Kate Sandeson
Set and Costume Design—Eric Bunnell
Sound Design—John Gzowski
Lighting Design—Rebecca Picherack
Fight Choreographer—Ryan Bondy

Characters

Patricia "Patsy" Hackett ....17 years old, candy striper.

Marie Anne Lussier .... 45 years old, pronounced "Marion." She is Matron of Arborfield Community Hospital. She is a chain-smoker, a coffee addict and puts salt on everything she eats.

Purificacion "Puring" Saberon .... 23 years old, Filipino Nurse from Daet, Camarines Norte, Philippines.

Indepencia "Penny" Uy .... 25 years old, Filipino Nurse from Quezon City, Manila, Philippines via California.

Charlie Govenlock .... 50 years old, caretaker of Arborfield Community Hospital.

Wilfred "Wilf" Klassen .... 25 years old, lab technician and goalie recruited from Uranium City to Arborfield Community Hospital to play for the Arborfield Flyers.

Dr. Miles MacGreggor .... 46 years old, Scottish ex-pat physician of Arborfield Community Hospital, a passion for all things fast and outdoors.

Setting

Arborfield Memorial Hospital.

November 1967.

Small rural hospital for the town of Arborfield, Saskatchewan—population 500.

Location: Hospital Common Room—two entrances, a kitchen, a table, a small couch, a bank of lockers, a chalkboard.

Performance Notes

... Denotes trailing off.

/ Denotes cutting off or overlapping.

Tagalog words and phrases are peppered throughout.

The play is in two acts.

Act I

Scene One: Welcome Nurses

MARIE ANN LUSSIER and PATSY HACKETT are in the Common Room. They hang up a sign which reads, "Mabuhay Nurses!" MARIE ANNE then paces the room, while trying to light her cigarette. PATSY goes to her portable record player and sifts through her personal record collection, looking for the best song for the festivities.

MARIE ANNE: Puri-fica-*ci-on*

In-de-pen-*cia*

Puri-fica-ci-on

In-de-pen-*cia*

In-de-pen-*cion*

PATSY: Marie Anne?

MARIE ANNE: Puri-fica-*cia*

In-de-pen-*cion*

Puri-fica-*cia*

In-de-pen-*cion*

PATSY: IndepenCIA.

PurificaCION.

MARIE ANNE: What? What did I say?

PATSY: IndepenCION.

PurificaCIA.

You were doing pretty good there for a while.

MARIE ANNE: Crap.

Puri-fica-*ci-on*

In-de-pen-*cia*

Why couldn't their mothers name them Sally and Jane and be done with it?

PATSY: Elvis! Perfect! Marie Anne, do you think they'll look like the hula dancers in *Blue Hawaii*?

MARIE ANNE: Mercy, Patsy, I don't know! They're from the Philippines, not Hawaii. Why are you just sitting around? Why aren't you helping your mom?

PATSY: The patients are all fed and the laundry is all folded. Anyway, she kicked me out of the kitchen because she's trying to perfect the fried rice recipe that Mrs. Chang gave her when we were over in Tisdale. Mrs. Chang says the girls will really like it. I don't know about that. Mom thought that the soy sauce was too expensive for something she wasn't going to use again, so she's using Lea and Perrins instead.

MARIE ANNE: That makes sense.

PATSY: Do you think they'll arrive with flowers in their hair and beautiful long dresses with flowers all over?

MARIE ANNE: Patricia Hackett! You've seen those girls in Nipawin and Carrot River. You act as if you've never seen a *Filipin-ese* before!

PATSY: Filipino. Not Filipinese.

MARIE ANNE: I'm losing my mind.

PATSY: Do you think it would be too weird if I hugged them when they got here?

MARIE ANNE: Lord, I don't know, Patsy. Why do you wanna hug them? They're grown women, they're not children.

PATSY: Well, I've been thinking. They've probably been in the airplane for a real long time. And they're a long, long way from home. If I had to fly halfway around the world to, say, Germany or Quebec or something, I sure would want a hug when I got there. Wouldn't you?

Enter WILF KLASSEN, toting goalie sticks and an enormous hockey bag.

MARIE ANNE: Wilf, you're late. There's a whole pile of samples waitin' for ya. You do know you are a lab technician, right?

WILF: *(Mumbles.)* Practice.

MARIE ANNE: Take that mask off!

WILF: *(Lifts the mask.)* Dr. Miles wanted to see it.

MARIE ANNE: Lord Almighty.

WILF exits.

PATSY: You know, Marie Anne, I think maybe you should try to not take the Lord's name in vain so much.

MARIE ANNE: Don't you get all high and mighty with me, Missy. You Hacketts swear like a bunch of drunken sailors. Makes me look like the Blessed Virgin Mary herself.

PATSY: Oh, and especially lay off the Blessed Virgin Mary. It's just that Mrs. Chang told me that Filipinos are very, very, very Catholic. More than us. More than the Irish even.

MARIE ANNE: Well, I'm French. So I trump them all. Anyway, that Wilf Klassen would make St. Francis himself swear up a storm.

PATSY: The Arborfield Flyers are 6:2 since he joined the team, Marie Anne.

MARIE ANNE: I don't care. He has a job to do and my tax dollars are paying for him to be a lab technician, not a star goalie.

PATSY: Charlie says in this town it's the other way around.

MARIE ANNE: Well, Charlie Govenlock would say that, wouldn't he? Where the heck is he? Leave it to Charlie to be the only person in the universe who can't spot two brown girls at the airport. I can only imagine.

Sound of a car pulling up.

PATSY: Oh my gosh. They're here! They're here!

MARIE ANNE: Oh Jes/ *(Jesus.)*

PATSY: Marie Anne! Don't curse!

MARIE ANNE: What? Geez Knees. I was going to say Geez Knees!

PATSY puts on her "Blue Hawaii" record selection, then runs to the door just as DR. MILES enters.

PATSY: Oh. It's only Dr. Miles. *(She stops the record player.)*

DR. MILES: Hello to you too, Poppet.

MARIE ANNE: Well it's about time, Miles.

DR. MILES: What's all the hoopla? Are you expecting the Pope?

MARIE ANNE: I've told you a hundred times. The nurses are arriving today.

DR. MILES: So?

PATSY: The nurses from the *Philippines.*

DR. MILES: Oh, right, right. Of course. What do you think, Patty-cake? You think maybe the girls can give me a couple of pointers on fishing? Maybe this year I can finally win something at the Pike Festival?

MARIE ANNE: When, pray tell, do you fancy they'll have time to fish, Miles? They've come here to be nurses. And if memory serves me correctly, you came here to be a doctor.

DR. MILES: A time to kill and a time to heal. For everything there is a season and a time to every purpose under heaven.

PATSY: Outta sight! I love that song. The Byrds, right?

DR. MILES: Ecclesiastes.

MARIE ANNE: It doesn't mean take off from work and hunt black bears, Miles.

DR. MILES: The Good Book is open to cultural interpretation, Marie Anne. Why else would there be five different churches in town?

MARIE ANNE: Tell it to the Marines.

PATSY: Ooh, the nurses will like that you can quote the Bible, I'm sure, Dr. Miles.

DR. MILES: And what about my dashing good looks, Patricia?

PATSY: Dr. Miles!

DR. MILES: I see you blushing, Marie Anne, so it must be true.

MARIE ANNE: Pfff!

DR. MILES: Where's Charlie? I want to show him my new gun.

MARIE ANNE: He's fetching the girls from the airport.

DR. MILES: Well, give me a shout when they get here. I'm just going to have a little wee kip in Examination Room Four.

DR. MILES exits.

MARIE ANNE: If you ask me, his licence should be revoked.

PATSY: He's a good doctor, Marie Anne, you said so yourself.

MARIE ANNE: I don't mean his doctor's licence. I mean his hunting licence. Maybe that way I can get him to do his job.

Sound of a car pulling up. PATSY runs to the window.

PATSY: It's them! They're here! It's really them! *(She plays the record again.)*

MARIE ANNE: Wilf! Miles! Get out here! The girls have arrived!

PATSY: Oh my goodness! They're sooooo cute!

MARIE ANNE: Patricia, you get away from that window. And mind yourself! They are not Kewpie dolls. They are nurses: mature, seasoned professionals.

Enter CHARLIE, PURING and PENNY. PURING is crying. CHARLIE is toting all of their bags, which are identical—they were provided to them by Canadian Pacific Airlines. CHARLIE is awkward and at a loss, PENNY is trying to comfort PURING, but is bad with intimate relationships in general. And crying. In general.

Son of a Perch, Charlie! What did you do?

PATSY: Marie Anne!

Hearing MARIE ANNE curse makes PURING cry a little bit harder.

CHARLIE: Nuthin! I didn't do anything. Everything was fine and dandy up until five minutes ago. She just started wailing.

MARIE ANNE: Maybe because you're two hours late and they're exhausted!

What in God's name took you so long?

CHARLIE: Well it took a while to find them. More than half the plane from Vancouver was Filipine-women/

MARIE ANNE/ PATSY: Filipino.

CHARLIE: Well no one told me!

PATSY: I told you they'd be homesick. (*She goes to hug PURING.*) Umm. Gosh. (*In a whisper.*) Marie Anne, how do you say it again?

MARIE ANNE: Mabuhay.

PATSY/
MARIE ANNE: Mabuhay!

CHARLIE: What's that mean?

MARIE ANNE: It means *welcome.*

PURING wails. PENNY stands beside her, exasperated and distracted.

CHARLIE: Told ya it wasn't my fault.

MARIE ANNE: Maybe we said it wrong.

PENNY: *Mabuhay. (ma-BOO-hi.)*

MARIE ANNE: Mabu-huh?

PENNY: *Hay. (Hi.)*

MARIE ANNE: Oh. Hi! Hello! I'm/

PENNY: It's *Mabuhay*. That is how it is pronounced.

MARIE ANNE: Oh! *Mabuhay.* Thank you/

PENNY: May I use your phone?

MARIE ANNE: Oh. Of course. Uh...uh...

CHARLIE: ...That one's Indepencia...

MARIE ANNE: ...Indepencia/

PENNY: Penny.

MARIE ANNE: No, dear, it's free. You don't have to pay a thing.

PENNY: My name is Penny. Everyone just calls me Penny.

MARIE ANNE: Penny? Well that's a relief. I mean. Penny! Penny. Of course. Penny. The phone is right over here. *(Penny glares.)* Or…why don't you use the one in the other room? Charlie'll take ya.

CHARLIE: Right this way, Penny.

CHARLIE and PENNY exit. PATSY tries to comfort PURING.

PATSY: Are you sick? Are you hungry? Do you miss your mom? Do you feel like throwing up?

MARIE ANNE: Maybe she's just tired.

PATSY: Are you scared? We won't hurt you. Promise.

PURING: Then why do you have a sign on the road that says,

"Welcome to Arborfield—The Land of Rape and Honey?!"

MARIE ANNE bursts out laughing.

MARIE ANNE: Oh, precious heart.

PURING: Puring.

MARIE ANNE: Sorry?

PURING: Puring.

MARIE ANNE: Purring? Who's purring? Patsy, did the Soucys' cat get in again?

PURING: I'm Puring. Short for Purificacion. My sister's name is Precious Heart.

PATSY: Who's more Catholic now?

MARIE ANNE: Mercy me!

PURING: Hello, Mercy.

MARIE ANNE: No. I'm Marie Anne. I was just...oh geez. Listen, honey/

PURING: And RAPE!

MARIE ANNE: Sweetheart, you misunderstood. Rape doesn't mean *rape.* Not that kind of rape. It's canola. It's a crop.

PURING: A crap?

MARIE ANNE: No, a crop. We harvest it. Like wheat. Or like rice. Arborfield is a sweet, harmless town, precious, I mean, Purific...ica...ica...

PATSY: Puring.

MARIE ANNE: Puring. No one here would hurt a fly.

Enter DR. MILES carrying a rifle and WILF wearing his lab technician coat and goalie mask.

PURING screams and faints into MARIE ANNE's arms.

What in the hell/

CHARLIE rushes back in.

CHARLIE: What's going on? Oh hey, Miles, is that your Winchester?

DR. MILES: Just like Marshal Matt Dillon! *(Holds up the gun.)*

Enter PENNY. Seeing DR. MILES with the gun, she screams and runs out again.

CHARLIE: I'll get her.

CHARLIE exits.

MARIE ANNE: Oh for Chrissakes, Miles. Would you mind being *a doctor* for a moment?

DR. MILES: What? Oh yes, right. *(Moves to help MARIE ANNE.)*

MARIE ANNE: PUT THAT GUN AWAY.

DR. MILES hands the gun to WILF. DR. MILES helps MARIE ANNE get PURING into a lying down position, on her back.

DR. MILES: Patty-cake, grab a pillow for her legs. Marie Anne, get her something cold for her head.

MARIE ANNE: I KNOW.

WILF: What can I do?

DR. MILES: Hold her head and make sure she's still breathing. I'll go get my kit.

Exit DR. MILES.

MARIE ANNE: *(Hands WILF a cold compress.)* Here Wilf, put this on her head.

Enter CHARLIE.

CHARLIE: I'm gonna need some help. She's gone and locked herself in the supply closet.

MARIE ANNE: Well, where are your keys?

CHARLIE: Don't work. She's barricaded it from the inside.

MARIE ANNE: Jesus, Mary and Joseph! What a mess! We've gone and nearly killed 'em and they haven't even been here for ten minutes.

MARIE ANNE exits with CHARLIE.

PATSY: Wilf? Is she still breathing?

WILF: *(Mask still on/muffled.)* No. Uh. I don't know.

PATSY: Don't you think you'd have a better idea if you took your mask off?

WILF: Right. I don't know.

PURING comes to. As she opens her eyes, the first person she sees is the dashingly handsome WILF. When she opens her eyes, WILF also is taken off guard. Love at first sight.

Hello.

PURING: Hello.

PATSY: *(Yelling.)* Marie Anne! She's alive!

Enter MARIE ANNE.

MARIE ANNE: Thank you, Jesus. Patsy, take her to her to the Nurses' Residence. *(To PURING.)* Dearest, I think you've had quite the day. Patsy'll show to your room and you just get settled and rest. We can start orientation tomorrow. Okay?

PATSY: Right this way.

MARIE ANNE: Wilf, make yourself useful. Grab her bags and bring them over to the residence. I'm going to see if Charlie has rescued the other one yet. Lord help us.

She exits. WILF gathers the bags. Since all the bags look alike, he assumes they all belong to PURING. He reads the tag.

WILF: In-de-pen-cia U-y, Que-zon City Manila, Philippines. *(Sigh.)* I think I love you.

He exits. Leaving one bag behind.

Scene Two: We're Different

Common Room, later that night.

PURING is cooking. She wears a Filipino house dress/duster (They look like mumus). PENNY enters, wearing a lovely modern housecoat. She has entered to retrieve her bag that was left behind.

PENNY: Oh, thank goodness. I thought I lost a bag. What time is it?

PURING: Here time or back home time?

PENNY: Here time.

PURING: Two in the morning. But ***tanghalian*** time back home. *(Snack time.)*

PENNY: No wonder. I'm starving.

PURING: I made chicken *adobo.*

PENNY: You made *adobo*?

PURING: Yes. Mrs. Lussier said that we could eat anything in the kitchen so...

PENNY: (*Opening a cupboard.*) Why didn't you just open a can of soup?

PURING: Why, when it's just as easy to make *adobo*? There was chicken in the fridge and vinegar and bay leaves and pepper...there was no soy sauce but I found this "Lea and Perrins" (*Pronounced literally*). It tastes almost the same. Anyway, the Campbell's soup is very expensive back home. I would hate to waste it.

PENNY: That's so provincial.

PENNY takes a can of Campbell's Chicken Soup. She rummages around the kitchen, with no consideration for PURING, finds a can opener and a pot. She opens the can, plops the contents into the pot, adds water and puts it on a burner.

PENNY: See? Simple. *(Beat.)* You're from Albay, aren't you? Saberon? That's your last name right?

PURING: No.

PENNY: Your name is not Purificacion Saberon?

PURING: Yes, it is. But no, I'm not from Albay. I'm from Camarines Norte.

PENNY: But you have relatives there, don't you?

PURING: Yes, but…

PENNY: Close enough.

PURING: Have you ever been there? It's not very close at all.

PENNY: There really isn't a need for me to leave Manila very much. We go north to Baguio in the summer. And I've never been west of Bulacan.

(Beat.)

It's freezing in here.

PENNY fetches her bags. She rummages through a suitcase and takes out a silk scarf.

PURING: That's a beautiful scarf.

PENNY: My auntie sent it to me. Pure silk. It's the new style. Everyone is wearing it in Glendale.

PURING: Glendale?

PENNY: Los Angeles? Hollywood? California?

PURING: I know where California is.

PENNY: I was there for two years nursing.

PURING: Is your *tita* nursing there now?

PENNY: No, my *aunt* has lived there for ten years. She's married to an American. I had plenty of admirers there. Glendale is so much better than this place.

PURING: Why did you leave?

PENNY: I didn't want to. My contract was up. They don't keep you for more than two years.

PURING: Maybe that's why this place is better. Can you believe? Permanent residency! Just for landing. And you can sponsor your family right away. My parents were very excited for me. Weren't yours? My classmate from nursing school said that her cousin came to Canada five months ago and already sent more than a hundred Canadian dollars back home for their family.

PENNY: My family doesn't need the money.

PURING: Well, if you don't need the money and you don't like it here, why are you here?

PENNY: That's none of your business.

PURING: Oh. Sorry. *(Beat.)* Your soup is boiling.

PENNY walks over to the kitchen. She notices PURING's shoes.

PENNY: What are those?

PURING: They're boots. I bought them during our stopover in Hong Kong.

PENNY: They're hideous.

PURING: They're fine.

PENNY: My flight stopped over in Tokyo. I am sure that if I saw you buying those in Hong Kong I would have stopped you. Of all the boots in the entire world, why would you buy those?

PURING: Because my classmate said that her cousin said that you need boots when you come to Canada because it is so cold that people lose their toes. And I don't care what they look like, they were inexpensive, and they are practical and I would rather keep my toes warm than fashionable.

PENNY: I would rather lose my toes.

PURING: Well I didn't ask for your opinion, did I?

PENNY: Typical.

PURING: What do you mean by that?

PENNY: You are just like the other girls I went to nursing school with who came from Albay.

PURING: I'M NOT FROM ALBAY!

PENNY: Close enough. (*She pours herself a glass of water and a helping of soup in a bowl.*) I'm going to eat in our room. It's too cold in here. Would you be a darling and bring my bag with you when you come in? My hands are full.

She exits.

PURING: *(Reading the tag on her luggage.)* Indepencia Uy, Quezon City Manila, Philippines. *(Scoffs.)* Typical.

Scene Three: Penny Is Not Puring

Common room, the following day. MARIE ANNE, PENNY and PURING enter. PATSY is in the room, folding laundry.

MARIE ANNE: So, that's the tour, gals, any questions?

PENNY: Yes, when do you pay us?

MARIE ANNE: What's that, P...p...p...

PATSY: She's Penny. And she's Puring.

MARIE ANNE: Right.

PURING: I think she asked where is the nurses' office?

MARIE ANNE: Oh. Right. Nothing fancy here, girls/

PENNY: *(Under her breath.)* No kidding.

MARIE ANNE: This room is pretty much it. It's our lunch room, office, and if we're overbooked we set up a hospital bed in here and push the table aside. That's only happened twice—three years ago there was a baby boom, on account of a particularly cagey winter. And last year there was a pile-up on Hwy 23. But they've since fixed the road, so's it shouldn't happen again. But I can't say the same about the baby boom. We'd have a better idea if only Wilf would pay more attention to his real job instead of hockey practice.

PURING: Hockey?

PENNY: Wolf?

MARIE ANNE: *Wilf* Klassen is our lab technician. Hockey is a stupid game. But you didn't hear that from me. That's the kind of blasphemy that'll get you tarred and feathered around here.

PENNY: What does that mean?

MARIE ANNE: Figure of speech. *(Beat.)* And that's that. So if it's all fine and dandy with you girls, here are your contracts to sign.

She hands them the contracts. PURING signs. PENNY examines it clause by clause.

PURING: Does Wilf Klassen work here every day?

MARIE ANNE: Every other day except weekends. At least, that's what I schedule him for.

PATSY: There's a tournament this week, Marie Anne.

MARIE ANNE: Christ Almighty, another one?

PURING twitches and gasps when MARIE ANNE curses.

PURING: Excuse me.

PURING exits.

PATSY: Aw geez, Marie Anne. You have to try to stop cursing.

MARIE ANNE: Sorry. I meant to say "cripes."

PENNY: Is a tournament bad?

MARIE ANNE: Well, it means don't expect Wilf any time soon.

WILF enters carrying a tray of test tubes. Upon seeing PENNY, who he thinks is PURING, he drops the tray.

MARIE ANNE: Oh my god. Those weren't the/

WILF: Uh, sorry.

PATSY: I'll help you clean it up.

MARIE ANNE: Wilf! Those weren't the pregnancy tests were they?

WILF: They were pregnancy tests?

MARIE ANNE: They were labelled.

WILF: Oh. Uh. Geez. Uh. I thought they were cholesterol tests. Which, um, if it helps at all, they all tested really high. Really high cholesterol. All of 'em.

MARIE ANNE: What am I supposed to do with that, Wilf? "Sorry, Mrs. Burkie, I don't know if you're pregnant, but you should really cut back on pork chops!"

WILF: Well, she is a little on the stout side…

MARIE ANNE: I've had enough of this. One more wrong step and I'm gonna have the hospital board ship you right back to Uranium City, tournament or not!

DR. MILES enters.

DR. MILES: Hey, Wilf! Good luck in the tournament. I have five clams running on you shutting out those bastards from North Battleford.

MARIE ANNE: Miles, I need you to deal with Wilf/

DR. MILES: Can't talk now, Marie Anne. Charlie just told me he spotted a family of vicious deer just outside of Zenon Park. Gotta protect the women.

PENNY: I beg your pardon?

DR. MILES: Deer! Dangerous creatures, Poppet. You never want to find yourself alone in the woods with one. To Dodge!

MARIE ANNE: Miles!

He exits. MARIE ANNE storms out after him. WILF clumsily tries to clean up the mess. He is beet-red embarrassed—being scolded in front of the woman (he thinks) he loves. PATSY sweeps up the mess and exits to get rid of it.

PENNY: I can't understand a word he is saying. Is he speaking English?

WILF: Uh…um…

PENNY: You hockey, don't you?

WILF: Uh. Umm. What's that?

PENNY: You hockey. You're supposed to be the lab technician but instead you hockey. Mrs. Lussier says it's stupid.

WILF: Uh. Umm. Yes.

PENNY: Well, if you also think it's stupid, then why do you do it?

WILF: Huh? Well, uh, no. Um. Yes, I mean…

PENNY: Do *you* speak English?

WILF: Yes. Yes. Umm. Uh. Yes. I mean, yes. I'm the hockey player. Goalie. Hockey is um, a noun. Not a verb. And I'm, I mean, hockey is not stupid.

PENNY: If you say so.

WILF: Umm. Uh. How are you feeling, Indepencia?

PENNY: Penny.

WILF: Penny? You're feeling Penny?

PENNY: Call me Penny.

WILF: Oh right! Ok. How are you feeling, Penny? I mean, from yesterday?

PENNY: Fine.

WILF: Oh. Good. Cuz, uh, we didn't mean to, uh, frighten you.

PENNY: I wasn't scared.

WILF: Oh! Um. Right. Maybe you were, um, low blood sugar sort of thing.

PENNY: I guess you would know.

WILF: Why's that?

PENNY: You are a lab technician.

WILF: Oh! Hahhah. That's a joke. Hahhah.

PENNY: Is it?

WILF: Uh…

PENNY: I need to use the phone.

WILF: Uh. Yes. Right over there.

PENNY: I know.

She checks the time, goes to the phone and dials. WILF remains, staring at her.

PENNY: Don't you have some tests to do?

WILF: Oh. Um. Yes. Right. Right…

PENNY: Goodbye.

WILF: Goodbye.

WILF exits.

PENNY: Hello. Operator? Please connect me with Manila, Philippines.

Enter PATSY.

PATSY: Hey, Penny.

Enter CHARLIE.

CHARLIE: Using the phone again, eh, Penny? You're like my youngest daughter, Cathy/

PENNY: Excuse me.

PENNY leaves.

CHARLIE: A little hoity-toity, that one. I like her.

PATSY: Can I tell you a secret, Charlie?

CHARLIE: Not if it's gonna get me in trouble.

PATSY: It won't.

CHARLIE: All right, then.

PATSY: I saw something yesterday.

CHARLIE: That's your secret? You saw something?

PATSY: I witnessed...magic.

CHARLIE: If you're smoking those hippie sticks, Patsy, I'm going to tell your ma.

PATSY: Geez, Charlie! I don't smoke grass!

CHARLIE: Good.

PATSY: Yesterday, when Puring came to...she looked at Wilf and Wilf looked at her and...fireworks!

CHARLIE: I don't get it.

PATSY: I think that Wilf likes Puring and Puring likes him back.

CHARLIE: That's trouble.

PATSY: No it's not.

CHARLIE: Yes, it is. Trouble with a capital T and a capital R.O.U.B.L.E, for that matter. Don't meddle, Patsy. I'm warning you.

Enter PURING.

PATSY: Oh hey, Puring. Sorry about Marie Anne's cursing. She don't mean anything by it. It's just her way of um, *emoting.*

CHARLIE: Oh, is that what it is? Lucky me. She *emotes* me very much.

PATSY: *(To PURING.)* Did you and Penny go to nursing school together?

PURING: No. I met her for the first time at the airport.

PATSY: In Manila?

PURING: No. In Saskatoon.

PATSY: That's *far out.*

PURING: Yes, it was a three-hour drive.

PATSY: No, not far out. *Far out.* Groovy. You never met before, but you look like sisters. It's, um, interesting, you know?

PURING: I don't think we look anything alike. Excuse me.

PATSY: What'd I say?

Scene Four: Puring Is Not Penny

A few days later. PATSY is folding laundry. Enter WILF, toting his hockey bag.

PATSY: How'd it go?

WILF: We won.

PATSY: Cool. How'd Hank play?

WILF: Palominos' defence cleared the puck, trying to grab a break for a shift change. They were tired. But I skated out and/

PATSY: Oh. Forget it. Don't tell me. I'll ask Hank myself.

WILF: Uh. Okay.

MARIE ANNE: *(Offstage.)* Judas Priest! What is that smell?!

PATSY: You better get to work. She's on the warpath today.

Enter DR. MILES in scrubs.

DR. MILES: Wilf.

WILF: Miles.

WILF exits. DR. MILES goes to his locker and starts to change out of his scrubs into hunting gear.

PATSY: Well?

DR. MILES: Oh! Patty-cake. Didn't see you there. Well what?

PATSY: Mrs. Laforge?

DR. MILES: It's a boy.

PATSY: Finally! Mr. Laforge will be so happy. Is Mrs. Laforge doing okay? Do you need me to do anything?

DR. MILES: Oh. She's fine, Patty. One of the new girls is taking care of it all. Can't talk. I'm taking an airplane up to Tobin Lake to shoot some ducks. Ducks!

Enter MARIE ANNE.

MARIE ANNE: Miles/

DR. MILES: Can't talk, Marie Anne. Must catch a plane.

MARIE ANNE: Miles, you need to have a serious conversation with Wilf. I've had it. The lab tests are piling up and/

DR. MILES: What am I supposed to tell him, Marie Anne? He's the best goalie the Flyers have had since/

MARIE ANNE: I don't give a flying fart about that, Miles. That doesn't give him the right to turn my lab into a locker room! The smell coming out of there, you'd think it was the morgue.

DR. MILES: We don't have a morgue.

MARIE ANNE: There will be when I murder him or drop dead from the stench!

DR. MILES: What do you want me to do?

MARIE ANNE: You're an educated man. Figure it out. Wilf! Get in here. Dr. Miles needs to speak to you.

DR. MILES: Marie Anne, I have to run/

Enter WILF.

WILF: Hey, Miles.

MARIE ANNE: Tell him.

MARIE ANNE exits. Enter PURING, unnoticed.

DR. MILES: Ah, cripes. Look, Wilfred. It's about the, uh, hockey.

WILF: We won.

DR. MILES: Who was it today?

WILF: P.A. Palominos.

DR. MILES: Way to whip the townies, Wilf! Good job!

Sound of a single-engine plane revving up nearby.

WILF: What did you want to tell me?

DR. MILES: Keep up the good work, son. This hospital is blessed to have you. Now, get back to work.

PURING: Excuse me, Dr. Miles. I am very sorry to interrupt you/

DR. MILES: Poppet! Good job in there. Gotta run.

PURING: But about Mrs. Laforgie's care plan/

DR. MILES: Top notch, poppet! I trust you. If you have any questions, just ask Marie Anne. I gotta catch the Duck Express before it flies without me.

DR. MILES leaves. She is left alone with WILF.

WILF: Uh. Um…

PURING: I better go check on the baby.

PATSY: Oh no! Wait. I'll go check on the baby. You should stay here. To uh, take a break.

PURING: But…

PATSY: Bye.

PATSY leaves.

PURING: Congratulations, Mr. Klassen.

WILF: Oh. Wilf. Just Wilf.

PURING: Congratulations, Wilf.

WILF: Umm. Thanks…For what?

PURING: You won?

WILF: Oh. Thanks. It was nothing.

PURING: Nothing?

WILF: Well, actually, it was kinda a big play.

PURING: What do you mean?

WILF: Well, the Palominos' defence cleared the puck, trying to grab a break for a shift change. They were tired. But I jumped out of the crease and picked the puck up and sent it across to Hank—risky pass, but the Palominos were trying to grab a shift change, not paying attention. Bang! Puck hits his stick and he goes across centre and in the zone on a break. He fakes left, switches over to his back hand, then…top shelf—where the peanut butter's kept.

PURING gives him a blank stare.

(Explaining it to her in bullet points.)

Grabbed puck

Crossed ice

Shift change

Top shelf

Peanut butter

Goal.

PURING: Hank could not reach the peanut butter?

WILF: Uh. There's no actual peanut butter. It's a saying. It means. Um. Well, basically, I helped Hank score a goal.

PURING: Oh. That was very generous of you.

WILF: Maybe you should just come see a game one day.

PURING: One day, maybe. Maybe when I am not working.

Beat. Beat. Beat.

WILF: Um. So. You helped deliver a baby today?

PURING: Oh. Yes. Mrs. Laforgie.

WILF: Laforge. It's French.

PURING: Laforge. Thank you.

WILF: *De rien.*

PURING: Bless you.

WILF: No. Uh. *De rien.* It's French, for "you're welcome."

PURING: Are you French, Wilf?

WILF: No. I'm from Uranium City….Uh. But my great-grandpa was Ukrainian. He came to work. And then he just, stayed.

PURING: Like me.

Beat. Beat. Beat.

Well, I should go check on Mrs. Laforge.

WILF: I should get back to work too.

PURING: Hockey work?

WILF: No. Hockey isn't work. It's fun. Lab work.

PURING: Not fun?

WILF: No. Not fun. But, at least now it's a bit, um, more interesting.

The phone rings.

PURING: I better go.

MARIE ANNE: *(From offstage.)* Wilf! You pick up that phone! You can do the explaining from now on!

PURING exits. WILF answers the phone.

WILF: Uh. Arborfield Memorial Hospital. Hello? Huh? I'm sorry, I can't hardly hear you. Who? From where? Uh. I don't know if I can accept the charges. Um… Hang on…

(Yells.) Phone call from the Philippines!

PENNY runs in and grabs the phone from him.

PENNY: Hello? Hello? There's no one there.

WILF: Oh. Must have hung up. Awful connection. Could hardly hear them.

PENNY: Did they say who was calling?

WILF: Um. I don't know. Maybe.

PENNY: Maybe?

WILF: They could have. Uh. Alls I could make out was Philippines. And he asked if I would accept the charges. I said I don't know about that.

PENNY: You should have said yes!

WILF: I guess so. But I'm in enough trouble as it is. You heard Marie Anne.

PENNY begins to dial the phone. WILF lingers.

PENNY: Don't you have work to do?

WILF: Oh. Right. Um. Right. Oh. I forgot to tell you. My next game is on Friday.

PENNY: What game?

WILF: Hockey.

PENNY: So?

WILF: Uh. Well, I just thought that maybe/

PENNY: *(Picks up the phone.)* Excuse me, Mr. Klassen, may I have some privacy, please?

WILF: It's just Wilf, remember?

PENNY: Wilf. Leave me alone.

WILF: Uh. Right. Sorry.

WILF leaves. Enter PURING.

PURING: There was a phone call from the Philippines?

PENNY ignores her.

PENNY!

PENNY: Yes, but that imbecile didn't accept the charges so I am calling back.

PURING: How do you know it was for you?

PENNY: Why would it be for you?

PURING: Why wouldn't it be for me? My family is there too.

PENNY: I'm sure they can hardly afford to call you.

PURING: Give me the phone.

PENNY: Hello? Operator? Please connect me with Manila, Philippines.

(To PURING.) I got here first. And I would like some privacy.

PURING: Penny! It could have been for me! What if it was an emergency?

PENNY: Then that giant would have said so. *(Into phone.)* Hello Manila, connect me with the Bonaventura residence in Makati, please. *(To PURING.)* Puring, leave me alone!

PURING hangs up the phone.

Puring!

MARIE ANNE enters.

MARIE ANNE: Did Wilf get the phone?

PENNY leaves in a huff.

Everything okay?

PURING: It's nothing, Mrs. Lussier. We're just a little homesick. That's all.

PURING exits. MARIE ANNE is left alone and checks the schedule. Enter DR. MILES.

MARIE ANNE: Miles. What happened to duck season?

DR. MILES: Tragedy. Missed the plane. *(Beat.)* No matter. I'm supposed to be at the Tisdale Hospital today anyway.

MARIE ANNE: Tisdale Hospital? What happened to Dr. Parker?

DR. MILES: Couldn't take the cold. Broke his contract and went home to tropical Toronto. Good riddance, I say! He actually told me he loathed the outdoors! So must be me to save the day.

MARIE ANNE: Don't give yourself airs. Are you scheduled to be there tomorrow?

DR. MILES: I'm afraid so.

MARIE ANNE: Well then, can you take Puring with you? It's her day off and apparently all the Filipino nurses from the nearby towns get together at Rose's Café on Friday.

DR. MILES: What about the other one?

MARIE ANNE: Penny? I don't know yet.

DR. MILES: Well…

MARIE ANNE: Can you drive Puring or not?

DR. MILES: That depends.

MARIE ANNE: On what?

DR. MILES: Which one is Puring?

MARIE ANNE: Miles, do you mean to tell me you don't know which one's which?

DR. MILES: I'm sorry, Marie Anne, I don't have that kind of memory. In my defence, I have always failed at names and memory games.

MARIE ANNE: It's a miracle you passed your medical exam.

DR. MILES: Marie Anne, anyone can tell a lung from a pancreas, a femur from a phalange. I think Florence Nightingale herself would have a challenge telling poppet from poppet.

MARIE ANNE: Penny and Puring!

DR. MILES: Admit it, Marie Anne, they're practically twins.

MARIE ANNE: ...

DR. MILES: Marie Anne?

MARIE ANNE: Okay, fine. Twins, no. Sisters, maybe.

DR. MILES: You can't tell them apart, either!

MARIE ANNE: That's not entirely true.

DR. MILES: Define entirely.

MARIE ANNE: I have a system.

DR. MILES: A system?! That's outrageous!

MARIE ANNE: Don't start, Miles. Who are you to judge?

DR. MILES: I'm not judging you, Marie Anne. I think it's outrageous you've kept your system a secret from me.

MARIE ANNE: Well, part of the system is the scheduling...

DR. MILES: Of course! How wickedly simple.

MARIE ANNE: Well, I'm the one making the schedule, but it becomes problematic when the schedule has to/

DR. MILES/
MARIE ANNE: Overlap.

DR. MILES: Ha!

MARIE ANNE: And then the system, well, it's more keeping an eye out for the subtleties.

DR. MILES: Clues! Very Agatha Christie of you, I'm impressed. Please enlighten me.

MARIE ANNE: Puring's nursing cap has a navy blue band, Penny's is black. Very hard to tell the difference in certain lights.

DR. MILES: That's useless for me. I'm as bad with colours as I am Filipinos.

Is that it, Miss Marple? Scheduling and nursing caps?

MARIE ANNE: Well, then there's the last resort. I'm right ashamed of myself, to be honest.

DR. MILES: What?

MARIE ANNE: When I curse, Puring has a... reaction.

DR. MILES: Allergies?

MARIE ANNE: No. She does this thing. This twitchy, gaspy thing. Hard to describe but you can't miss it.

DR. MILES: Do you mean to tell me, Marie Anne Lussier, Head Nurse of Arborfield Memorial Hospital, that you curse on purpose to trigger convulsions in a girl as a means of identification?

MARIE ANNE: It didn't start that way, but in desperation, it is the quickest way to figure out who's who.

DR. MILES: Forget the rest of your system, Marie Anne. That one's a winner.

MARIE ANNE: Miles, you can't shoot your mouth off hoping it will land. It's not target practice. You could give her a heart attack.

DR. MILES: Or perhaps she'll think I'm so full of sin that she'll pray for my soul and I'll get a free ticket into that heaven of yours, Marie Anne. Consider how many extra prayer points you're earning every time you swear in Puring's presence. It's better than going to church!

MARIE ANNE: I'm not proud of it, Miles. It's not a game. You have to promise/

DR. MILES: I'm just teasing you, Marie Anne. For what it's worth, you're a kind-hearted woman, God-fearing or not. It'll be a last resort.

Enter PENNY. DR. MILES is inspired to test out "The System."

MARIE ANNE: Miles.

DR. MILES: I promise.

Scene Five: Letters

The following evening. PURING is alone, surrounded with piles of letters. She is writing. PATSY enters.

PATSY: Oh. Hi, Puring. I didn't think anyone was here. Are you off tonight?

PURING: No, I am working the night shift. Why are you here so late?

PATSY: I'm here all the time. Haven't you noticed?

PURING: Yes. But I did not want to assume. I thought that you were a volunteer.

PATSY: Yeah. That's why I work so much. Cuz it doesn't cost anybody anything to have me around. What are you doing, I wonder?

PURING: I finished writing the patient reports. So I thought I'd catch up on writing home.

PATSY: All this?

PURING: Yes.

PATSY: Wow, Puring. You sure write a lot of letters.

PURING: I have a lot of family.

PATSY: All this is for your family?

PURING: Yes. Most of it. My mother and father, my brothers and sisters. And my cousins. And my aunts and uncles. Plenty of family. And some friends from nursing school. They all want to know how I am doing. Look at this.

She opens an envelope and it is filled with soil and sand.

PATSY: It's full of dirt!

PURING: My brother Emile gave it to me when I left home. He was afraid that there was only snow here and nothing else. So he gave me soil in case I missed it.

PATSY: Do you miss it?

PURING: What? Soil? There's lots of soil here. He's just silly.

PATSY: Do you write to your boyfriend?

PURING: My boyfriend?

PATSY: Was that an inappropriate question? Marie Anne is always telling me to *be appropriate* around you and Penny. I'm sorry/

PURING: I have never had a boyfriend.

PATSY: Oh.

PURING: Do you have one?

PATSY: Um. Sorta. Almost. I mean, I really, really admire Hank Meeks. But he's not my boyfriend. I'm not sure if he likes me in that way.

PURING: Oh. I see.

PATSY: Hank is Wilf's best friend. They're on the same hockey team.

PURING: Oh.

PATSY: Sometimes I like to go watch a game. You should come. You know. For fun.

PURING: Maybe. For fun.

Beat.

PATSY: How come you don't just call the Philippines instead of writing?

PURING: It is very expensive to call the Philippines from here.

PATSY: Penny does it all the time.

PURING: Maybe she has more money than I do.

PATSY: Oh.

PURING: Anyway. I like letters. They are more special. I can read them over and over again. You can't do that with a phone call.

PATSY: It must be hard to be so far away.

PURING: Yes. But I am the oldest in my family and they need me to be here.

PATSY: My two older brothers, John and Peter, work up in the rigs in Alberta. I haven't seen them for almost a year now. They make money there to send home so we can buy equipment for the farm. I miss them.

PURING: We are the same.

PATSY: Yeah. I guess so.

She hands her some paper and a pen. They write in silence.

Enter WILF.

WILF: Uh, hello.

PURING: Oh! Wilf Klassen!

PATSY: Hey, Wilf. What a coincidence! I was just saying that you and Hank are on the same hockey team and that we should watch you guys play some time.

WILF: Uh, well, Hank just dropped me off. He's still outside. He said if you were still here to ask you if you wanted a lift home.

PATSY: Really?

WILF: Yeah.

PATSY: Great! I mean, yes! I mean, I better go!

PURING: Maybe I think this Hank admires you, too. Goodnight.

PATSY exits.

WILF: I'm interrupting you. Sorry.

PURING: No. No. You are not interrupting. I am just writing a letter. I finished the patient reports already.

WILF: You don't have to explain to me. I'm not a snitch.

PURING: Snitch?

WILF: I won't tell Marie Anne on ya. Get you in trouble. I'd never do that.

PURING: There is no trouble. There is no work to be done. There are only two patients here tonight. I will check on them soon.

WILF: Who you writing to, I wonder?

PURING: No one. No one special. Just my sister. She was having difficulties in her new school.

WILF: Boy trouble? Hahaha.

PURING: She is seven years old.

WILF: Right.

PURING: I didn't know you were working tonight.

WILF: Yeah. I sorta made a deal with the hospital auxiliary; if I can squish all my hours in over the next few days, I can play in the tournament this weekend. I think they only said yes cuz the tournament is at our arena, so's it's not like it's a big road game or anything, which is kinda dumb cuz it's not like it's any easier playing at home, especially when you got those crazy jerks from Jordan River chucking alfalfa pellets at the net. There was this one time... Sorry, I'm boring you. I should get to work.

PURING: Don't apologize. It is very interesting.

WILF: You should. Uh. Come. On Sunday. To the game. I'm sorry. I keep hounding you. I mean, I keep asking you.

PURING: I don't/

WILF: S'okay. I know. You're working.

PURING: No. I am not. I was just planning to go to mass.

WILF: Game's not until two. Father Doucette is the referee, so's he has to be there. I guarantee mass'll be real fast on Sunday. And Patsy'll be there on account of Hank, so's you won't have to sit by yourself. It'll be fun. Or you know, uh, good. Or you don't have to, too. That's okay/

PURING: I think I will come/

WILF: Or not. Or. Oh. Okay. Great. Great.

PURING: Great.

Beat. Beat. Beat.

Then the faint sound of a baby crying.

PURING: I should go and check on the baby/

WILF: Baby. Okay.

PURING: Okay. I'm going. Now. To check. On the baby.

WILF: Okay.

PURING: Okay. Bye.

WILF: Bye. For now.

PURING: For now.

PURING exits. WILF sighs. He picks up the phone. Dials "0."

WILF: Uranium City. *(Beat.)* 937-2645. *(Beat.)* Hi, uh, Donna. It's me. Can you talk? I'm sorry to call so late. I just wanted to tell you I can't come up this weekend. The hospital is making me work overtime. Yeah. And on top of that I have a game on Sunday, so, you know. Of course. I miss you too. *(He hears someone coming.)* Look, Donna, I should go. I'm supposed to be working. Sorry to wake you up. I'll figure out something soon. *(Hangs up.)*

WILF exits. PENNY enters from the nurses' quarters. She picks up the phone.

PENNY: Hello? Operator? Please connect me with Manila, Philippines......... Hello, Manila? Please connect me with the Bonaventura residence in Makati. Romi? ***Si Penny 'to. No. Hindi 'to*** collect. (*It's Penny. No. This is not collect.*) ***Ano'ng oras na diyan?*** *(What time is it there?)* ***Merienda*** time? What are you eating? Just tell me. Because I miss it. I have to cook my own food here, and you know that I can hardly cook rice. ***Suman and manga?*** Mmmm. What else? ***Bibingka?*** I wish I was there.

I hate it here. ***Hindi nga.*** No one can hear me. Even if they could, they can't understand me. We are speaking Tagalog. ***Oo,*** they are nice enough. But I don't care about them. I am here to work. I don't have to be their friend. Anyway, they all look the same to me, it is hard for me to tell them apart.

CHARLIE enters, unseen by PENNY. He pours himself some coffee. He's not intentionally eavesdropping, but he likes PENNY so much and finds the melody of her voice entertaining.

PENNY: I have saved up about $50 so far. I will go to Saskatoon to make the arrangements when I can. It is three hours away. ***Hindi ito*** Quezon City. I don't have a driver. What? ***Saan ka pa punta?*** *(Where are you going?)* Where do you have to go? Fiesta? Oh. Sounds like you are having a wonderful time. Don't go. I don't care if your mom is coming. You can't keep me a secret for… Romi? Romi?

CHARLIE: Bad connection?

PENNY screams.

Sorry, Penny. I didn't mean to scare ya. I have to stop doing that. But I didn't want to interrupt you. That Filipino language of yours sure is pretty. Sounds like music. Can't understand a word of it, mind you. 'Cept Saskatoon. But I don't s'pose there's a Filipino word for that, eh? Wanna cuppa joe?

PENNY: Excuse me.

CHARLIE: Are ya working?

PENNY: No.

CHARLIE: So's you don't need to rush off, do you?

PENNY: I didn't know you worked at night.

CHARLIE: Snow was coming down so I came to shovel the driveway and the walk.

PENNY: So late?

CHARLIE: The snow ain't on a schedule, so neither am I. Here. Grab a seat. I have this orange that I can't eat all by myself. You don't have to talk to me, you can just eat.

PENNY goes to sit next to him. He slowly begins to peel the orange.

I ever tell you 'bout my youngest? Cathy? She's gone and married now, lives over in Nipawin. Married to the most boring fella in the world, if you ask me. He's a veterinarian. But can't bait a hook to save his life. So's can't talk fishing with the guy. And he don't have time to play hockey or curl. Anyway. You remind me of Cathy. She was always on the phone with her girlfriends before she married Tom. Alls her friends live down the street but she'd rather talk on the phone than pull her boots on to walk down two houses. Don't tell anyone, but I loved listening to her talk. Couldn't understand a word she said, talking a mile a minute with her girlfriends. But in a way, kinda sounded like music. I miss it.

PENNY: I wasn't talking to my friend.

CHARLIE: I didn't think so.

They continue to eat the orange in silence.

PENNY: Did you object to their marriage?

CHARLIE: Who? Cathy and Boring Tom?

PENNY: Yes.

CHARLIE: Well, he's as dull as a log, but he's the only vet between here and Prince Albert, so's he makes a good living. And she loves him. Lord knows why.

PENNY: Love can be unreasonable.

CHARLIE: I take it your folks don't approve of your fella.

PENNY: They do not know about him.

CHARLIE: Ah, I see.

PENNY: And he has not told his parents about me.

CHARLIE: That's a pickle. How long you been together?

PENNY: Four years. It's very…complicated. We were engaged just before I went to California, three years ago. When I returned to Manila, his parents forbid the marriage.

CHARLIE: Why?

PENNY: They don't have to give their reasons. As long as he is dependent on them, he must do as they say. So I looked for a way that he didn't have to be dependent on them.

CHARLIE: And that's why you're here.

PENNY: Yes. I need only to file the papers in Saskatoon and he will be here in a month. *(Beat.)* We have been apart more than we have been together. And when we are together, we argue about how long we have to be apart again. I miss when it was simple. Like…it doesn't matter.

CHARLIE: Course it does. What do you miss?

PENNY: When he was courting me he used to give me little presents and tell me I was beautiful all time. I miss those little things.

CHARLIE: Penny, men are stupid.

They continue to eat in silence until they finish the orange.

PENNY: Thank you for the orange, Mr. Govenlock. Oranges are my second-favorite food.

CHARLIE: What's number one?

PENNY: Mangoes.

CHARLIE: Never heard of 'em.

PENNY: They are heavenly. My family owns a plantation back home.

CHARLIE: Then I'll have to take your word for it.

PENNY: I think I better go to bed.

CHARLIE: You know Penny, I'll be heading down to Saskatoon on Friday, to run some, you know, uh, errands. Long drive. *(Looks at the chalkboard/ schedule.)* Says here you have the day off, maybe you'd like to keep me company?

PENNY: Thank you, Mr. Govenlock. I think I would.

Scene Six: Penny Melts With A Mango

The next day. PENNY enters, removing her coat, followed by CHARLIE, who is carrying a number of Eaton's packages. PATSY, having heard them pull up, runs into the room to meet them.

PATSY: What'd you get? What'd you get?

CHARLIE: Calm yourself, Patsy! Make yourself useful and take these boxes, would you?

PATSY: Oh, Penny! I'm so jealous you went to Eaton's. I've only been twice. It's one thing to admire all of the clothes and things in the catalogue, but a whole other thing to browse through in real life.

PENNY: I didn't go. The packages are for Mrs. Lussier.

PATSY: You didn't go to Eaton's!? Oh Penny! Eaton's is a cultural institution. You simply must go to Eaton's. You haven't *lived* if you haven't gone to Eaton's. All the way to Saskatoon and not go! That's practically a sin.

CHARLIE: Don't listen to her, Penny. You don't want to get corrupted by her waning sense of religion.

Enter MARIE ANNE.

MARIE ANNE: There you are, Charlie. How was the drive?

CHARLIE: No complaints. Good company.

MARIE ANNE: Oh, yes. Did you enjoy the trip, dear? Charlie didn't bore you to death?

PENNY: It was pleasant, thank you.

MARIE ANNE: Good, good. (*To CHARLIE.*) Where's the other one?

CHARLIE: Dunno. Was in Saskatoon, remember?

MARIE ANNE: Right. Right. Well, if you're done in here, can you help me lift Mr. Ellis into bed?

PATSY: I can help.

MARIE ANNE: No, Patsy. He's…in a state. Best leave it to Charlie and me.

PATSY: Was he passed out in front of the pool hall again?

MARIE ANNE: Never you mind. Go find out if your ma needs help with the dinner rounds.

PATSY: Aww…

MARIE ANNE: Come on.

PATSY and MARIE ANNE leave.

PENNY: Thank you, Charlie.

CHARLIE: Oh, quit it, Penny. You've thanked me enough. So what's next?

PENNY: Waiting.

CHARLIE: Don't get discouraged, Penny. Be patient.

PENNY: Thank you, Charlie. You are kind.

CHARLIE: Tell that to Marie Anne.

MARIE ANNE: *(From offstage.)* Charlie! Get the frick in here!

CHARLIE exits. Enter WILF from the outside, carrying a small paper grocery bag. PENNY "in her civvies," is wearing a flattering modern dress. WILF is caught off guard.

WILF: Oh! Umm. Hello.

PENNY: Hello.

WILF: Didn't expect to see you here.

PENNY: Where should I be?

WILF: I mean, um. Today.

PENNY: Why is that?

WILF: It's your day off.

PENNY: How did you know that?

WILF: Oh, um, the schedule. And you told me.

PENNY: I don't recall.

WILF: Oh, well. Maybe I'm wrong. You, um, look different.

PENNY: What do you mean?

WILF: I mean, um, swell.

PENNY: I do not know that word.

WILF: You look, if you don't mind me saying, beautiful.

PENNY: Beautiful?

Beat. Beat. Beat.

WILF: Pretty. I mean, pretty…different. It's…uh… just pretty…different to see you not in your uniform and all. Just, um, unexpected. That's all.

PENNY: Why? Do you wear your hockey outfit all the time?

WILF: Hahah. Oh. Uh, no. That would be rude, I think.

PENNY: Rude?

WILF: Cuz it really smells. Nobody should be subjected to that torture. *(PENNY steps back.)* Oh, no. I don't mean now. And my gear is in my bag. And I always shower after practice. And games. So I mean I don't smell. Now. Or ever. Except right after the game. But not now. Really.

PENNY: If you say so. Goodbye. *(She turns to leave.)*

WILF: So anyway, I got you this.

PENNY: What is it?

WILF: It's a little gift, sort of. I picked this up for you at Chang's grocery. Was passing through Tisdale this morning. Thought you might like it, Mrs. Chang said all the Filipino nurses love 'em. I was gonna give it to you tomorrow or Sunday. Cuz I didn't think I'd see you today. Being your day off and all. And Mrs. Chang said it will taste better tomorrow or Sunday, but seeing as I'm seeing you right now, I best give it to you now and you can decide which day is better. Well, anyway. Here you go.

He hands her the paper bag. She opens the bag.

It's a mango.

PENNY: I can see that.

WILF: *(Dejected, turns to leave.)* Well, there you go.

PENNY: Wilf?

WILF: Uh-huh?

PENNY: Thank you.

WILF: *De rien.*

PENNY: Bless you.

WILF: *De rien*. French. For "you're welcome." Remember?

Enter MARIE ANNE.

MARIE ANNE: Oh well, there you are, Wilf. Thank you for showing up to work only thirty minutes late.

WILF: Uh. *De rien?*

MARIE ANNE: Don't get cheeky.

PENNY: It means you're welcome.

MARIE ANNE: I know, dear. I'm French. *(To WILF.)* One more time, Wilf, and I'm docking your pay. Now that you're here, I want to talk to you about those latest samples.

WILF: Don't worry, Marie Anne. I did 'em. All of them tested negative—not one of them is pregnant.

MARIE ANNE: Well, that's good news.

WILF: It is?

MARIE ANNE: I'm sure that Mrs. William, Mrs. Jordan and Mrs. Leland will be very relieved to know that their *husbands* are *not* pregnant.

WILF: Oh. Um. Sorry? *(MARIE ANNE turns to leave.)* Where are you going?

MARIE ANNE: I'm going to step outside for a moment to scream. May I suggest that you get your butt into that lab and retest those samples as labeled, *for gallstones,* before I wring your neck?

WILF: Uh/

MARIE ANNE: NOW!

MARIE ANNE exits.

PENNY: Wilf?

WILF: Yeah?

PENNY: *Salamat.*

WILF: Huh?

PENNY: It means "thank you."

From offstage we hear MARIE ANNE scream, followed by muffled swearing.

WILF exits. PURING enters from the outside.

PURING: Oh. There you are. Where were you today?

PENNY: Saskatoon.

PURING: I didn't know you were going.

PENNY: Mr. Govenlock was running errands. He asked me to keep him company.

PURING: We were wondering where you'd gone.

PENNY: Who is *we*?

PURING: Today was the get-together with the other Filipino nurses.

PENNY: Oh. I forgot.

PURING: This is the second time you forgot. (*Beat.*) I heard that Saskatoon is lovely and that there is a Filipino grocery store there.

PENNY: Who told you that?

PURING: Millie Estoya. She and Letty Camposano work in Carrot River. And I met Rose Welchman. She lives in Nipawin.

PENNY: Welchman is not Filipino.

PURING: Yes she is. She is married. To a farmer in Nipawin.

PENNY: A Filipino and a Canadian? Falling in love?

PURING: What? You think it's impossible?

PENNY: No. Not impossible...perhaps irresponsible.

PURING: What do you mean by that?

PENNY: Well, their poor children! They will be sadly unattractive.

PURING: Penny!

PENNY: It's true. They will be giants with enormous feet and mismatched eyes. One blue. One brown. You watch.

PURING: That is unkind.

PENNY: It's true.

PURING: It's not. You don't know. Rose is beautiful. And you haven't met Herman/

PENNY: HERMAN?! Well, now, of course their children will be ugly! His name is Herman!

PURING: You shouldn't be so judgmental. It's very un-Christian.

PENNY: You shouldn't be so naïve. It's very provincial. *(Beat.)* Oh well. Love can be unreasonable.

PURING notices the mango.

PURING: What's that?

PENNY: A mango. Obviously.

PURING: Where did you get it?

PENNY: At the Chinese grocery store in Tisdale.

PENNY exits.

PURING: I was there all afternoon. I didn't see you there.

PURING follows PENNY. PATSY enters. She folds laundry. Enter WILF.

PATSY: Wilf.

WILF: Patsy. *(Beat.)* Um, can I ask you something?

PATSY: What?

WILF: Well, it's uh. Well, there's a guy on the team…

PATSY: Who?

WILF: It's not important.

PATSY: If I guess, will you tell me?

WILF: No.

PATSY: Is it Hank?

WILF: No. No.

PATSY: Are you sure it's not Hank?

WILF: No! I mean, yes, I'm sure it's not Hank. Quit it. The name's not important. It's about the situation. Not the person. Okay?

PATSY: Okay, fine.

WILF: This guy, um, is really screwing up plays cuz he's distracted all the time by this girl…

PATSY: Hank said that Coach doesn't let girls watch you guys practice.

WILF: No. We don't. This guy, he keeps thinking about her.

PATSY: What about her?

WILF: Uh. I don't know. It's just, a problem. He's not focusing on the ice and he also can't sleep and can't focus on his work either. That's what he tells me.

PATSY: Is she a good kisser?

WILF: What?!

PATSY: Is. She. A. Good. Kisser?

WILF: He hasn't kissed her.

PATSY: What's he waiting for?

WILF: I don't know. I don't think she knows that he's thinking about her.

PATSY: I don't get it.

WILF: He, uh, said he hasn't told her. She doesn't know that, he, um, likes her. In that way.

PATSY: Oh. So. Why doesn't he just tell her? Or ask her to go for a soda or something?

WILF: Cuz he's scared.

PATSY: Is it Sid Rio? It's Sid Rio, isn't it? Hank said he has it bad for Helen Soucy in Zenon Park. I'm right, aren't I?

WILF: Forget it.

PATSY: Hang on! What about the guy?

WILF: I'll figure it out.

PATSY picks up WILF's slip of the tongue, but doesn't call him on it. Instead…

PATSY: You know, Wilf, I think you should tell your buddy that if he's too scared to talk to her, he should put it in a letter.

WILF: Put what in a letter?

PATSY: His deep longing and admiration for the girl of his dreams, of course.

WILF: That's sissy.

PATSY: It's romantic.

WILF: Same difference.

PATSY: Well, I was talking to one of the nurses/

WILF: Which one?

PATSY: It's not important.

WILF: What did she say?

PATSY: Well, let's just say that she thinks letters are way more special than phone calls.

WILF is baffled by this seemingly very complicated riddle. PATSY shuffles through drawers. She hands WILF an envelope, paper and a pen.

WILF: What's this for?

PATSY: Give it to your friend. Just in case.

She leaves. WILF makes a decision. He makes sure he is alone. He sits at the table and begins to write.

WILF: Dear Penny…You are so beautiful.

He can't continue. Stuck for words. He flips through PATSY's record collection. Makes a selection and is inspired.

I…want…to…hold…your…hand.

He stops. Goes to the phone and dials.

Operator?…Uranium City.

Scene Seven: The Mail

Saturday evening. MARIE ANNE is waiting. Enter CHARLIE.

MARIE ANNE: Christ on a cracker, Charlie, did you get lost on the way home from the post office? It's nine o'clock!

CHARLIE: After Gib gave me the mail she guilted me into swinging by the Legion to help set up for the Meat Draw tonight. You know ya can't say no to Gib, or you'll never see the mail again.

MARIE ANNE: Well, come on. I need you to help me move the beds in Room Three.

CHARLIE: I gotta sort the mail.

MARIE ANNE: Now, Charlie.

MARIE ANNE exits. Enter DR. MILES.

CHARLIE: Drat. *(Beat.)* Miles? Sort the mail for me?

DR. MILES: What's in it for me?

CHARLIE: My gratitude.

DR. MILES: And a bucket of bait?

CHARLIE: Miles, it's November. You know it's not fishing season, right?

DR. MILES: The fish don't know that.

CHARLIE: I'll see what I can do.

They shake on it. CHARLIE exits. DR. MILES goes to mail slots, but then is struck by a better idea.

DR. MILES: MAIL!

PENNY and PURING enter. DR. MILES immediately gets overwhelmed. He squints to look at their hats. He panics. The girls look at him expectantly.

DR. MILES: Oh, ladies, uh. I apologize in advance…

PENNY and PURING stare, confused.

Jesus Christ.

PURING reacts.

Ah. Puring! This one's for you, and this one, and this one… *(Continues on, distributing about eight letters.)* And this one's for you, Penny. And this one. And that's it. Would love to talk, poppets, I mean Penny and Puring.

DR. MILES goes to his locker and grabs fishing gear.

Oh, look at the time. I should go do my rounds. Lots of work to do. Must keep busy.

DR. MILES exits with fishing gear.

PENNY: Honestly, I can never understand a word he says. Can you?

PURING: I have a system.

PENNY: Huh. *(Beat.)* You got a lot of mail today.

PURING tears into a package. Dried mangoes.

PURING: Would you like some dried mango?

PENNY: Who sent this to you?

PURING: *Tatay*. He used to buy these for me after Sunday mass when I was a little girl. *(Beat.) Tatay* won't write; my *lola* says that he is too emotional. So he sent me these. I wish he would write. But this is the best he can do.

PENNY: At least you know your father is thinking of you.

PENNY opens and reads her letter (not the one from WILF).

Ay Dios. *(Oh God).*

PURING: What is it?

PENNY: It is a letter from Romi.

PURING: Who's Romi?

PENNY: My fiancé.

PURING: I didn't know you are engaged.

PENNY: I am.

PURING: It must be hard to be apart from him.

PENNY: It is...for me. I call him and tell him that I miss him. But he hardly has time to talk because he is running out the door. It is partly because of the time difference but...still...

PURING: He has written you a letter. Surely he misses you too.

PENNY: All he has written about is the latest cock fights/

PURING: He is a gambler?

PENNY: No. He breeds them.

PURING: That is his job?

PENNY: That is his pastime. His family is wealthy. He doesn't need a job. *(Beat.)* Oh well. ***Nagtatampo lang ako.*** I'm just sulking. I'm sure when he gets here it will all be fine. I have filed the papers to sponsor him over. If all goes well, he should be here in four weeks.

PURING: It will certainly be hard. There isn't any work in town to be had.

PENNY: What do you mean?

PURING: Haven't you noticed all the men in town just hanging around? Mrs. Lussier said that after the harvest, there isn't any work for them. Not until the spring.

PENNY: We aren't going to stay here.

PURING: What? You have to. We both agreed to stay here for two years.

PENNY: You did. Not me.

PURING: We signed the identical contract, Penny. I was with you.

PENNY: Well, if you are staying here, that is your plan. Not mine. As soon as Romi gets here, we are getting married and moving to Vancouver.

PURING: You can't leave. It's not right.

PENNY: Don't judge me, Puring. You are no different.

PURING: What do you mean? I signed that contract and I mean to honour it. I'm not leaving.

PENNY: And after two years, are you going to sponsor your *Nanay* and *Tatay* and brothers and sisters to live here? You said so yourself, there is no work for them here. You know as well as I do that come the end of your contract, you will be on a bus or a plane to somewhere else.

PURING: You don't know anything about me.

PENNY: I know enough. You're just mad because I'm right. *(PENNY opens WILF's letter.)* Excuse me, I have my rounds.

PENNY exits. PURING has an outburst of anger. Enter WILF.

WILF: Uh. Hello.

PURING: Oh, Wilf. Excuse me. I didn't know you were there.

WILF: You okay?

PURING: I'm fine. I'm fine. How are you?

WILF: I'm happy…to see you. Are you sure you're okay?

PURING: I'm fine. It's just that the mail came and/

WILF: Oh. Um. A letter?

PURING: Yes and well/

WILF: You didn't like, um, the letter?

PURING: It's not that/

WILF: Well, uh. You're obviously upset. I didn't think that would happen. I should go. I'm sorry.

PURING: You don't have to go, Wilf. Would you like some dried mango?

WILF: Uh, sure. You really like this stuff, eh?

PURING: It is my favorite. I like it more than fresh mango.

WILF: Oh, sorry. I'll know that for next time.

PURING: You are always saying sorry, Wilf. There is no reason.

WILF: Sorry.

PURING: Stop saying that word. Just eat.

WILF eats the mango.

PURING: It's good?

WILF: Mmm-hmm. Delicious.

PURING: ***Sarap.*** *(Delicious.)*

WILF: Syrup? No. It kinda tastes like licorice.

PURING: I don't know what that is.

WILF: I'll bring you some. Sometime.

PURING: I forgot to tell you. I really enjoyed watching your hockey game the other day.

WILF: Thanks for coming. Again.

PURING: It is very entertaining. Everyone is so excited and emotional.

WILF: How come you didn't say hello after the games?

PURING: I didn't want to bother you.

During this next exchange, they get closer.

WILF: No. Never. You would, um, never be bothering me. (*Under his breath.*) I meant what I wrote.

PURING: What's that?

WILF: Uh, well, um. Have you heard the Beatles?

PURING: Oh yes. I saw them in concert in Manila.

WILF: Really? They went to the Philippines?

PURING: Yes, they've been all over the world.

WILF: Not here.

PURING: Maybe not yet.

WILF: What is your favorite song?

PURING: Hmm. "Twist and Shout." I like to dance. Do you like them, Wilf?

WILF: Uh, yeah. They're okay.

PURING: What is your favorite song?

WILF: I didn't have one before. But now I do.

PURING: What is it?

WILF: "I Want to Hold Your Hand."

He reaches for her hand. He squeezes it and they linger for a bit. In spite of herself, she pulls away. Overwhelmed, PURING exits.

Oh crap. I'm an idiot.

PENNY enters with WILF's opened letter.

Oh, Penny, I'm sorry, I didn't mean to upset you, I just wanted to/

PENNY: Hold my hand?

WILF: Uh, yes. I'm sorry.

PENNY: And you bought me a mango.

WILF: Yes, I'm sorry, I didn't know it was the wrong kind/

PENNY: And…the other day you said I was beautiful. Did you mean it?

WILF: I think that you are just the prettiest, most lovely, beautiful gal I've ever ever met.

PENNY steps towards him and kisses him.

End of Act I.

Act II

The scene begins exactly where the previous scene left off. WILF and PENNY in a kiss. They break apart abruptly and awkwardly. Both are obviously bewildered at the lack of "magic." Something is just not right. Enter CHARLIE. They jump apart.

CHARLIE: Penny. Wilf.

WILF: Charlie!

PENNY: Hello, Mr. Govenlock.

Excuse me. *(Leaving.)*

CHARLIE: Sure thing. Hey, did Miles give you the mail?

PENNY: Yes. I. Well. Excuse me. I really must…

PENNY exits. WILF and CHARLIE are left in an awkward moment.

WILF: I should be going, too.

CHARLIE: Nice girl, that one.

WILF: What's that?

CHARLIE: Penny. Nice girl. Reminds me of my youngest. Cathy. You remember her. Chatterbox. Always in everybody's business.

WILF: Right. Cathy. I should go.

CHARLIE: Pull up a chair. Have some coffee. What's your rush? How's the team doin'?

WILF: We're number two going into the tournament in two weeks.

CHARLIE: Good on you. How's Donna?

WILF: What's that?

CHARLIE: Donna. Your fiancée.

WILF: Who told you about/

CHARLIE: Cathy.

WILF: Cripes.

CHARLIE: You know she's engaged, hey?

WILF: Cathy?

CHARLIE: Penny, Wilf. Penny is engaged.

WILF: ENGAGED?! To who?

CHARLIE: Fella in the Philippines.

WILF: She didn't...I mean, she never...I mean, engaged?! Are you sure?

CHARLIE: Sure's I am that you're engaged. You are engaged, aren't you?/

WILF: Well/

CHARLIE: Cathy has a tendency to exaggerate. But I'm thinking, you know, when it comes to being engaged, ya are or yer not/

WILF: But/

CHARLIE: I may not be some rootin'-tootin' goalie or test-tube tinkerer but when it comes to bein' promised to marriage, well, seems pretty straightforward to me. And I'm not gonna stand by while you take advantage of that sweet pretty girl.

WILF: I wasn't taking advantage/

CHARLIE smacks him.

Hey!

CHARLIE: I'll make it simple for you. She. Is. Engaged. She's saved every penny she's earned to bring that fiancé of hers over from the Philippines.

WILF: Penny's saving pennies?

Smack.

CHARLIE: Are you listening to me?

WILF: When?

CHARLIE: When what?

WILF: When is he coming?

CHARLIE: It don't matter! You're engaged, too!

WILF: But/

Smack.

Ouch! Geez, Charlie!

CHARLIE: Hate to say this, Wilf. Because I think you're a pretty swell goalie. But if I catch you anywhere near her again, I'm going to break both your legs.

WILF: But…

Threat of a smack.

WILF: OK!

Enter PATSY.

PATSY: Charlie. Wilf.

CHARLIE: Hey.

WILF: Hey.

PATSY: What'd I miss?

WILF: Nuthin.

CHARLIE: Nuthin.

PATSY: Aw. Come on, really?

CHARLIE: Nuthin.

PATSY: No one tells me anything.

CHARLIE: Nuthin to tell. Right, Wilf?

WILF: Nuthin to tell.

PATSY: Marie Anne is looking for you, Charlie.

CHARLIE: I already moved the beds. What does she want me for now?

PATSY: Find Dr. Miles.

CHARLIE: Again?

PATSY: Yup.

CHARLIE: Any leads?

PATSY: Nope.

CHARLIE: Right. Tell her I might be awhile.

CHARLIE goes to his locker. After much fussing, retrieves a flashlight and exits.

PATSY: So, really. What'd I miss?

WILF: Leave it, Patsy.

PATSY: What?

WILF: I mean it. You've ruined my life.

PATSY: What? What'd I do?

WILF: This is all your fault.

PATSY: The letter?

WILF: You knew it was me?

PATSY: Wilf. I'm a professional.

WILF: Write a letter, you said. She'd love it, you said.

PATSY: She didn't? Wait. What did you write? Did you write something goofy? No offence, but you don't have the most romantic vocabulary in the world/

WILF: Geez, will you just shut up for a minute already!

PATSY: You don't have to be so mean about it, I just wanna help out.

WILF: I don't want your help.

PATSY: Gosh, Wilf, you look like you need to barf…did you inhale something gross in the lab?

WILF: My brain hurts.

PATSY: Have you been forgetting to wear your mask during games?

WILF: No. Gimme a minute, would ya?

PATSY lingers, staring at him impatiently.

PATSY: Are you better now?

WILF: Patsy!

PATSY: Hey, maybe, just maybe, the letter didn't work because well, because of the language barrier? Maybe she prefers letters in Tagalog.

WILF: I'm leaving.

PATSY: Wait, Wilf. You don't have to tell me what you wrote, though I imagine it wasn't very eloquent. But that's not your fault. Well, you could tell me what you wrote, if you want, and I could tell you how it sounds to a girl, you know/

WILF: It doesn't matter what I wrote or how it sounds or what she thought of it. None of it, okay, Patsy? She's engaged. End of story.

PATSY: What are you talking about?

WILF: She's engaged. To a guy from the Philippines. She sponsored him over. And I'm just stupid. That's all.

PATSY: No she's not.

WILF: She is, Patsy. It's not up for debate.

PATSY: But that's impossible. She's never even had a boyfriend.

WILF: Well, maybe it works different over there, I don't know.

PATSY: What did she tell you?

WILF: She didn't tell me. Charlie did.

PATSY: What does Charlie have to do with it? You should ask her yourself! I'm sure you're wrong.

WILF: I can't talk to her, Charlie will kill me.

PATSY: Why?

WILF: Cuz I kissed her.

PATSY: YOU KISSED HER?

WILF: Yeah.

PATSY: Fireworks?

WILF: Not. Exactly. Augh, Patsy. This is all sissy talk. I got work to do.

PATSY: No fireworks?

WILF: See ya, Patsy.

PATSY: Not even a spark?

WILF: I gotta go.

PATSY: Wait! Hang on!

WILF: I got work to do. Don't follow me.

PATSY: But/

WILF: I mean it!

WILF storms out.

PATSY: Oh wow, wow, wow.

Enter DR. MILES.

DR. MILES: Wow is right, Patty-cake! Nighttime is the right time for fishing!

PATSY: Can't talk now, Dr. Miles. I have to find Puring.

DR. MILES: What's your hurry, Patty-cake? Surely you have two minutes to appreciate the bounty that my rugged angler talent has yielded.

PATSY: You know it's not fishing season, right, Dr. Miles?

DR. MILES: And hence even more reason for you to be in awe of my abilities!

These beasts put up quite a fight, but I bested them all!

PATSY: *(Peeking into his cooler/bucket.)* They look kinda small. My little brother caught a whole bunch like that but my dad made him throw them back in.

DR. MILES: *(Hurt.)* Did you say you have to be somewhere?

PATSY: I gotta find Puring. If you see her before I do, can you tell her I'm looking for her?

DR. MILES: What's it worth to you?

PATSY: Dr. Miles! It's an emergency!

DR. MILES: A matter of life and death?

PATSY: Sorta.

DR. MILES: It doesn't sound like quite the emergency you think it is. However, I might be persuaded if someone were to impart a *sincere* appreciation for my sportsmanship. Now, honestly, take a look at these fish again. Wouldn't you say they are the biggest fish you ever laid eyes on?

PATSY: Fine! Yes, they are giant fish and you are a great fisherman!

DR. MILES: Why thank you, Patty-cake. I will tell Poppet that you are looking for her if I see her.

PATSY: Puring.

DR. MILES: That's what I said.

PATSY: You better get rid of your gear. Marie Anne is pretty mad. She sent Charlie after you.

PATSY exits. DR. MILES proceeds to his locker to stash away his fishing gear. As he does this, PENNY tentatively and cautiously enters the room, not seeing DR. MILES. To make room for his fishing rod, he removes his rifle from his locker. As he does this, he notices PENNY.

DR. MILES: Ah, Poppet! You are wanted/

PENNY, who has a hard time understanding DR. MILES, screams and runs away.

Oh cripes, not again. (*After her.*) It's not loaded this time!

He fumbles to stash the gun and quickly removes his fishing wear to reveal his scrubs underneath. As he does this, MARIE ANNE enters.

MARIE ANNE: What on earth?

DR. MILES: Ah, Marie Anne. There you are! I've been looking all over for you.

MARIE ANNE: I heard a scream!

Enter WILF.

WILF: Someone screamed?

DR. MILES: I didn't hear a thing. Must be the wind.

MARIE ANNE: Where on earth have you been, Miles?

DR. MILES: Been here all along, Marie Anne.

Enter PURING.

DR. MILES: Ah, Poppet! I meant to say Patsy is looking for you. Said it's a matter of life and death.

MARIE ANNE: Don't pull that bullroar with me!

DR. MILES: No word of a lie, she said it was an emergency.

MARIE ANNE: You have NOT been here all along. I sent Patsy to send Charlie to look for you.

PURING: Where is Patsy?/

WILF: Charlie's back?

PURING: Excuse me/

WILF: Sorry/

PURING: As you were saying/

WILF: What did you say?

DR. MILES: Patty-cake went that-a-way.

MARIE ANNE: Charlie went out looking for Miles.

WILF: Oh good.

MARIE ANNE: What is that? *(Pointing to bucket/cooler of fish.)*

DR. MILES: No idea.

WILF: It's a bucket of bait.

DR. MILES: Wilf, I believe it is time we get your eyes checked. But not now, I must do the rounds.

MARIE ANNE: Look in on Mr. Ellis first.

DR. MILES: He's here again?

MARIE ANNE: Yes.

DR. MILES: All right, Marie Anne. Lead the way.

MARIE ANNE and DR. MILES exit, leaving PURING and WILF alone.

WILF: I should go.

PURING: Wilf. About earlier.

WILF: Forget it.

PURING: Forget it?

WILF: Yeah. Forget it. I gotta go.

PURING: But, Wilf/

WILF: Aw, geez. You know, I can't believe it. Do I have the word "sucker" written across my forehead?

PURING: There is nothing on your forehead.

WILF: I sure feel like a sucker.

PURING: Is that good?

WILF: Sucker. Fell for it. Idiot. Shoulda known better. Shoulda known that a beautiful gal like you was just toying with me.

PURING: You think I'm beautiful?

WILF: You know I do!

PURING: No. I do not.

WILF: I don't know what it's like in the Philippines, but around these parts we'd call that leading a guy on.

PURING: I'm confused, Wilf Klassen.

WILF: ME TOO!

Enter CHARLIE.

WILF: Charlie!

CHARLIE: That Miles is nowhere to be found.

WILF panics, as he doesn't want CHARLIE to slug him for talking to "Penny."

WILF: I gotta go.

PURING: But you were saying/

WILF: Nothing. I was saying nothing. Uh, only talking about the lab tests. Yup. Lab tests. Official work. Nothing else. Um. Bye.

WILF exits.

PURING: He did not mention lab tests.

CHARLIE: That Wilf is an odd pickle, Puring. Sometimes I wonder if he's had way too many pucks to the head.

PURING: Is that what you call a sucker?

CHARLIE: Ha! Good one! Well, that was a waste of time.

PURING: Dr. Miles returned a few minutes ago.

CHARLIE: I figured. Did he catch anything?

PURING: I think so, over there.

CHARLIE glances into the bucket/cooler.

CHARLIE: Nope. If anybody's looking for me, Puring, tell 'em I went to the rink. But if they're *really* looking for me, I'll be in the cellar listening to the game.

CHARLIE exits. PATSY enters.

PATSY: Puring! Thank goodness! I've been looking all over for you.

PURING: Who is dying?

PATSY: Dying? Someone's dying?

PURING: Dr. Miles said something about an emergency. And death. I am ashamed that I cannot always understand when he speaks so fast.

PATSY: You and me both.

PURING: So you are not hurt?

PATSY: No.

PURING: Is someone dying?

PATSY: No. It's not that kind of emergency.

PURING: What kind then?

PATSY: I need you to talk to Wilf.

PURING: Wilf? Why?

PATSY: Well, we were hanging out and he was telling me about…you know…how he *feels*…

PURING: How he feels?

PATSY: Yeah. Uh, kind of intimate feelings, you know about…

PURING: Intimate?!

PATSY: Yeah. So I helped him relieve those feelings by /

PURING: / You…helped Wilf Klassen relieve his intimate feelings?

PATSY: Yeah.

PURING: Patsy, where I am from that is a very serious thing.

PATSY: It was no big deal. I was just trying to help out. Cuz *you* know, it's a good thing.

PURING: It is?

PATSY: Oh. Love is always a good thing.

PURING: You call it love?

PATSY: Oh, yes. It sure is! But now I'm kinda in trouble.

PURING: Trouble?

PATSY: Yeah, but I know I can fix it.

PURING: Fix it?

PATSY: I just need you to talk to him.

PURING: Oh, no, no, no. Patsy, I am so sorry but I cannot help you. This is just, oh dear. This is too much. I must. I think I need to lie down.

PATSY: But you have to/

PURING: I must go, Patsy. *(Beat.)* I will pray for you.

PURING exits.

PATSY: Oh crap. I think I just made things worse. Crap. Crap. Crap. *(Beat.)* Calm down, Patsy, calm down. You can fix this. You can fix this. I can fix this!

She gets an idea. PATSY madly searches around the common room and finds a piece of paper and a pen. She writes.

Dearest Puring…I need to talk to you.

She looks at the schedule.

Meet me in the Common Room at 11 o'clock.

Signed, *(Scratches that out.)*

Sincerely, *(Scratches that out.)*

Love, Wilf

She puts the letter in an envelope.

WIIIILLLLLFFFFF!

Enter WILF wearing lab gear.

WILF: What?

PATSY: Hey.

WILF: What is it Patsy? I'm busy.

PATSY: Are you still mad at me?

WILF turns to leave.

Wait!

WILF: I got work to do, Patsy.

PATSY: Yeah, I know. But um, Hank called.

WILF: I didn't hear the phone ring.

PATSY: I mean, I called Hank.

WILF: So?

PATSY: He told me to tell you that he's gonna pick you up tonight cuz he needs to go over some plays.

WILF: Tonight?

PATSY: Yeah. Said for you to meet him here at 11.

WILF: That doesn't make any sense. We already went through the plays this afternoon at practice.

PATSY: Yeah. Well, he said that um, it was the only time he could reserve the rink. So…

WILF picks up the phone.

What are you doing?

WILF: I'm calling him.

PATSY: You can't.

WILF: Why?

PATSY: Cuz it's late and you might wake up his mom.

WILF: It's not *that* late.

PATSY: Yes it is. She's been sick and going to bed early.

WILF: How do you know?

PATSY: Hank said. He said to tell you not to call him back because his mom's going to bed. Just be back in here by 11, would you?

WILF: Geez. Fine. Is that it?

PATSY: Yes.

WILF: Can I go back to work now?

PATSY: Yes. Be back by 11.

WILF exits.

(Yelling after him.) Don't forget!

Enter MARIE ANNE.

MARIE ANNE: Patsy, would you quit yelling? You're going to wake up the patients.

PATSY: Sorry, Marie Anne.

MARIE ANNE: Don't say sorry, just don't do it. Listen, I need you to go down the street and tell Mrs. Ellis her husband is here again and she needs to bring him home.

PATSY: Now? It's late?

MARIE ANNE: No. Yesterday. Now, Patsy, now. Do you have something better to do?

PATSY: I just have to give this to Puring.

MARIE ANNE: Give it to me. I'll give it to her.

PATSY: Are you sure?

MARIE ANNE: Yes.

PATSY: It's really important you give it to her, Marie Anne. Okay?

MARIE ANNE: Yes, for goodness sake, Patsy. Now skedaddle!

PATSY reluctantly gives the letter to MARIE ANNE. PATSY exits. PENNY enters.

Oh, hello, dear. I was just about to go looking for you.

PENNY: Charlie is looking for you.

MARIE ANNE: What now?

PENNY: He wants to know where you want him to put Mr. Ellis.

MARIE ANNE: Put Mr. Ellis? What's wrong with his room?

PENNY: He ran out of his room and Charlie found him in the cold cellar going through the bins of margarine.

MARIE ANNE: Land's end, not again. I really need a vacation. *(She turns to leave.)* Oh, before I forget, here. *(Hands PENNY the letter.)* And if Patsy comes back with Mrs. Ellis tell her to keep her entertained for a bit.

MARIE ANNE exits. PENNY opens the letter.

PENNY: Dearest Puring….11 o'clock…Wilf. *(Beat.)*

Dearest Puring?

Love Wilf?

PURING?

Enter PURING.

PURING: Yes?

PENNY: *(Hides letter.)* Nothing.

PURING: You said my name. What is it?

PENNY: Nothing. I was just reading the schedule. *(Beat.)* You look tired.

PURING: I am. This evening has been stressful.

PENNY: You are working the night shift.

PURING: Yes. At 11 PM.

PENNY: Why don't we switch? I can work your shift tonight. You can rest and take my morning shift.

PURING: But that means you will be working a double shift.

PENNY: It's fine. It's been a slow day for me. I am not tired.

PURING: Well, if you don't mind. That would be very helpful. Thank you, Penny. Thank you for being so considerate.

PENNY: No problem.

PURING: If you change your mind, I will just be at the residence.

PENNY: Have a good rest.

PURING exits. Enter PATSY.

PATSY: Hey, Penny.

PENNY: Where's Mrs. Ellis?

PATSY: She's not coming. She wants to hit him with a frying pan. *(Beat.)* Are you just finishing up?

PENNY: No. I am working tonight.

PATSY: Tonight? As in tonight tonight?

PENNY: Yes.

PATSY: I thought it's supposed to be Puring.

PATSY runs to the chalkboard.

Says here that it's supposed to be Puring.

PENNY: She was not feeling well so I am working for her.

PATSY: No. You can't work for her!

PENNY: Why not?

PATSY: Because. Because, well, aren't you tired? You've been working all day long. Surely you're tired.

PENNY: I'm not.

PATSY: Then I should work instead.

PENNY: You are not a nurse.

PATSY: I'm a Candy Striper, it's close enough.

PENNY: No. You are in high school. I am a nursing graduate from the University of Santo Tomas. It is not "close enough."

PATSY: Right. *(Beat.)* Did you ask Marie Anne if you can work?

PENNY: No. Why should I?

PATSY: Cuz you might be working overtime for the week and if you are working overtime that'll cost the hospital more money and maybe Marie Anne might be mad if she has to pay out more than she's supposed to.

PENNY: I doubt she will be mad.

PATSY: But you can never be too sure. And you don't wanna risk getting her mad, do you? Not to mention in trouble with the hospital board for overspending. That would be just awful. Better to avoid the mess and let me work instead.

PENNY: I'll tell her when I see her.

PATSY: You should go tell her now.

PENNY: Why?

PATSY: Because…because she should know right away so she can change it on the board.

PENNY: I'll change it myself.

PATSY: NO!

PENNY: Why?

PATSY: She's very particular about her schedule. She likes to make the changes herself. Something about the continuity of penmanship. Better to tell her now and let her change it on the schedule herself.

PENNY: Fine. I will go find her.

PATSY: Now?

PENNY: Yes. Now.

PATSY: Yes. *(Beat.)* And take your time.

PENNY exits. Enter DR. MILES.

DR. MILES: Where are you running off to?

PATSY: I have to find Puring.

DR. MILES: Still? I know she's tiny, Patty-cake, but the amount of times you lose her is frankly irresponsible.

PATSY: I didn't lose her. I just…gotta fix something.

DR. MILES: Well, best of luck to you. And though I adore you, please don't ask for my help. I am tuckered out and need to lie down for a wee kip before the night shift.

PATSY: Working a double?

DR. MILES: Feels like a quadruple.

PATSY: Why don't you lie down in room four?

DR. MILES: Mr. Margarine.

PATSY: Right. *(She looks at her watch.)* Can you be done your nap at eleven?

DR. MILES: What's in it for me?

PATSY: Really?

DR. MILES: Really.

PATSY: Fine! What do you want?

DR. MILES: Be a sweet pea and check my bear traps outside?

PATSY: You put bear traps outside the hospital?

DR. MILES: Only in front of the shed. Didn't want them to get at my ducks. Ducks!

PATSY: Augh. The things I do. If I die checking your traps, it's on you.

DR. MILES: Good thing I'm a doctor. And dim the lights before you leave?

PATSY: Just in case you see Puring before I do, tell her to meet me here at 11, okay?

DR. MILES: Poppet at 11. 10-4.

PATSY dims/turns off the lights and exits. DR. MILES lies down on the couch and pulls a blanket over his head. Enter PENNY. She stumbles in the dimness and makes her way across the room towards the light switch beside the other entrance. On her way, she trips and falls into the couch—on top of the covered DR. MILES.

PENNY: ***Aray!*** *(Ouch.)*

DR. MILES: Poppet?

PENNY: Ahhh!

PENNY is terrified. In fear and panic she socks DR. MILES in jaw.

DR. MILES: Oww!

PENNY hits him so hard that when he speaks the words are slurred and in pain.

DR. MILES: Poppet! It's me! It's just me!

PENNY: YOU! AGAIN!

DR. MILES: Calm down, Poppet! I didn't mean to frighten you.

PENNY: SPEAK ENGLISH!

Enter PURING, holding a letter in her hand.

PURING: ***ANO ITO?!*** *(What is this?!)*

PENNY: ***Ano? Ha?*** *(What?)*

(Grabs the letter.) ***Sino ka ba!*** *(Who do you think you are?)* That is none of your business! Why were you going through my things?

PURING: I was writing a letter and you left it open on our desk!

PENNY: You had no right/

PURING: ***Galing kay*** *(It is from)* Wilf Klassen!

PENNY: ***Wala yan.*** *(It's nothing.)* It's stupid.

PURING: HE WANTS TO HOLD YOUR HAND!

PENNY: He's mistaken.

PURING: You are engaged! Why does he want to hold your hand?!

PENNY: He is a big oaf. I don't know why he writes these things.

PURING: *(He is a.)* Casanova ***siya!*** A Don Juan!

PENNY: ***Pwede-ba.*** *(Hardly.)*

PURING: You don't know what he's been doing! I can't believe him! ***Walang Hiya!*** *(Shameless.)* Wilf and you! You and Wilf!

PENNY: Wilf and me, ***wala*** *(Nothing.)* Nothing happened with Wilf! He is a lovesick puppy.

PURING: ***Ay Dios Ko!*** *(Oh my goodness.)* First Patsy and now you!

PENNY: Patsy? ***Ano?*** *(What?)*

PURING: I have to do something! I have to…to…tell someone….

PENNY: Wilf kissed Patsy too?

PURING: YOU KISSED WILF KLASSEN?

PENNY: ***Hindi.*** *(No.)*

PURING: You just said!

PENNY: ***Sabi ko*** *(I said)* nothing.

PURING: You are engaged! You cheated on Romi!

PENNY: ***Hini ko siya ki-niss.*** *(I did not kiss him.)*

He kissed me. I did not kiss him.

PURING: What?!

PENNY: I mean, nothing happened, it was a misunderstanding, an accident/

PURING: How do you accidentally kiss someone?

PENNY: ***Para ka'ng jealous.*** *(You're acting jealous.)*

PURING: I am not jealous.

PENNY: Are you sure?

PURING: Wilf Klassen is a despicable human being! I am not going to let him stay here and continue to take advantage of poor, innocent women.

PURING grabs the letter from PENNY.

PENNY: Give that back!

PURING: No! It's evidence!

PENNY: ***Sira ba ulo mo?*** *(Is your head broken?)* It belongs to me.

PURING: What do you care? ***Sabi mo*** it's stupid. ***Sabi mo*** he's an oaf.

PENNY: GIVE IT BACK!

PURING: NO!

A ridiculous chase ensues.

DR. MILES: Oh dear. This isn't going to turn out well. Ladies! Please!

DR. MILES tries to interrupt the chase and is knocked down. PURING stuffs the letter into her uniform. PENNY tackles her. CHARLIE and MARIE ANNE enter.

CHARLIE: Now, now. This is no way to behave.

MARIE ANNE: What in Heaven's name is going on?!

DR. MILES: No idea. They're talking in Filipino. But boy, is it dramatic!

CHARLIE: Like I tell my own girls, ain't no excuse for you young ladies to act like your ma never taught you better.

MARIE ANNE: Miles!

DR. MILES: Don't "Miles" me, Marie Anne. I am an innocent bystander.

MARIE ANNE: Then why are you on the ground?

DR. MILES: I got caught up in the Poppet stampede.

PENNY: She attacked me!

PURING: Everything that comes out of your mouth is a lie!

MARIE ANNE: Calm down, girls. Calm down.

PENNY: She stole my personal property!

PURING takes out the letter and throws it at her.

PURING: Take it. I don't need it. This isn't about you, anyway. You are hardly innocent.

PENNY: You should talk!

PURING: What does that mean?

MARIE ANNE: What is that? *(Referring to the letter.)*

PENNY: *(Rips up the letter.)* Nothing. Nothing at all.

CHARLIE: Well, now, Penny. How's about you and me take a little walk and cool off, whatta ya say?

MARIE ANNE: That's a very good idea.

PENNY exits. Charlie follows.

DR. MILES: By the way, Puring, Patsy was looking for you.

PURING: Poor Patsy!

MARIE ANNE: Patsy? What is going on?

PURING: Mrs. Lussier, there's something I need to tell you. It's important. And confidential.

DR. MILES: Don't mind me.

PURING: Can we go somewhere else?

MARIE ANNE: Before you say anything, let me have a cigarette. I have a feeling that I'm gonna need it.

Exit MARIE ANNE and PURING. Enter PATSY.

DR. MILES: Bears?

PATSY: Nope.

DR. MILES: Bollocks.

PATSY: Puring?

DR. MILES: She went that-a-way. You sure missed a wonderful hullabaloo.

PATSY: Huh?

DR. MILES: Can't talk Patsy, must get to it, lest I dare the wrath of Maid Marion.

DR. MILES leaves.

PATSY: Oh my gosh! It's almost 11!

Enter WILF toting his hockey bag, wearing his goalie mask on his head.

Wilf!

Where are you going?

WILF: Are you kidding me? Hank?

PATSY: Uh. Oh! Right! He was here and then he left because, uh, he forgot his skates and said he'll be right back. So stay here.

PATSY is slowly walking toward the same exit that PURING used.

WILF: Where are you going?

PATSY: I, uh, um, just forgot to tell Mr. Ellis that Mrs. Ellis isn't coming.

WILF: I just passed by Room Four. He's sound asleep.

PATSY: Yeah, well, I should at least, um, leave a note, in case he wakes up and wonders why he's not in his own bed at home. DON'T GO ANYWHERE.

WILF: When Hank gets here we gotta take off, Patsy, so's not to lose ice time. So if you want to see him, hurry up.

PATSY: Ice?

WILF: The rink.

PATSY: Right! Ice! Good memory, Wilf. Don't go anywhere.

PATSY exits. PENNY enters from the opposite door; she is carrying her luggage.

WILF: Penny! Uh, you going on a trip?

PENNY: I'm leaving. I'm going to Saskatoon. I can stay here no longer.

WILF: Look, Penny, about earlier…when I…I mean, when you and I…when our…or rather when we…

PENNY: Honestly, Wilf, sometimes I wonder if English isn't your first language.

WILF: This is a bit hard to explain. You see, earlier, when I um…we kissed/

PENNY: That did not happen.

WILF: Yes it did. We were standing right here. You were holding the letter I wrote you.

PENNY: I don't know what you are talking about.

WILF: Here. You. Me. Letter. Kiss.

PENNY: Perhaps you are thinking of someone else. *(She hands him the PATSY-written letter.)*

WILF: Dearest Puring…Common Room…Eleven o'clock…Love Wilf…P…P…P…

PENNY: Puring!

WILF: I didn't write this!

PENNY: Likely story.

WILF: I DIDN'T!

PENNY: Save your lies, Mr. Klassen.

WILF: Lies? You should talk. You led me on all this time/

PENNY: I did no such thing/

WILF: Coming to my games and all/

PENNY: Games? What games?/

WILF: And kissing me when all this time you are engaged!

PENNY: Yes, I am engaged. And we never kissed. Nothing happened between you and I. Nothing. And now I am leaving. Goodbye, Wilf.

As she attempts to exit, WILF stops her by grabbing her suitcase.

Let go of my bag!

CHARLIE: Wilf.

WILF: Charlie.

CHARLIE enters. Seeing what appears to be WILF grabbing PENNY, he slugs WILF.

WILF: Ow!

CHARLIE: I told you to stay away from her!

PENNY: Mr. Govenlock!

CHARLIE: No need to thank me, Penny.

WILF: I was just trying to talk to her, Charlie!

CHARLIE: More like grabbing!

Enter MARIE ANNE, who immediately walks right up to WILF and slaps him.

WILF: Ow!

MARIE ANNE: You're lucky I don't break your legs! You're fired! I want you out of here now!

WILF: Fired! What I do?/

CHARLIE: What he do?

MARIE ANNE: Don't play stupid with me, Wilf Klassen! You're lucky I don't call the police!

WILF: What are you talking about?

MARIE ANNE: Everyone else in this place may think you're a hero. How dare you take advantage of those girls!

WILF: What?

CHARLIE: What?

CHARLIE slugs WILF. He is knocked to the ground again.

WILF: OWWWW! Charlie!

PENNY: Charlie! Stop it!

MARIE ANNE: Don't defend him, Penny. He deserves it, after how he romanced you and Puring/

CHARLIE: PURING?

PENNY: PURING!

WILF: PURING?/

MARIE ANNE: And what he's done to Patsy! *(She begins to weep.)*

CHARLIE/ WILF: PATSY?!

CHARLIE: What he do?

WILF: I DIDN'T DO NOTHING TO PATSY!

MARIE ANNE: I don't know what I'm going to tell her mother! She's probably going to have to leave town, who knows when she'll be able to come back. "Hire Wilf Klassen," everyone said "best goalie this town'll ever have," you all said. Well, I hope you're happy!

CHARLIE: Leave town…he didn't…no…not Patsy…

MARIE ANNE: Yes! Yes, Patsy!

CHARLIE: MILES!

MARIE ANNE: What's Miles got to do with it?

CHARLIE: I'm going to need his gun.

WILF: Charlie, Marie Anne, calm down a minute. I don't know what you're talking about!

CHARLIE: Miles! Get in here!

Enter DR. MILES.

DR. MILES: What's all the commotion?

CHARLIE: Where's your gun?

DR. MILES: In my locker.

WILF: What the hell?

MARIE ANNE: I've fired Wilf. He's leaving.

CHARLIE: Not before I kill him.

WILF: HAS EVERYONE LOST THEIR MIND?

DR. MILES: You lose a game, Wilf?

PENNY: I knew you kissed Puring!

DR. MILES: Not that I am aware of.

PENNY: Not you. Wilf.

WILF: No!

PENNY: And you kissed Patsy, too?

MARIE ANNE: If only it was just kissing!

DR. MILES: What did you do to Patty-cake?

WILF: Just kissing? Wait, what do you think I did to… you think me and Patsy? You mean you think Patsy and me, uh, uh, umm/

MARIE ANNE: Yes! You and Patsy uh-umm'd!

WILF: Why in the world would you ever think that! I've never…I wouldn't…how could you even think/

PENNY: You kissed me and then you kissed Puring and then you kissed Patsy?

WILF: NO! I ONLY KISSED YOU!

MARIE ANNE: Poor poor/

Enter PATSY.

CHARLIE, MARIE ANNE and DR. MILES speak the next three lines together.

CHARLIE: Patsy!
MARIE ANNE: Patsy.
DR. MILES: Patty-cake!

WILF: Patsy! Thank God. Tell them!

Tell them you and I have never, and will never…kiss/

PATSY: Ew!

WILF: Ew?

PATSY: Kissing you would be like kissing my brother. Disgusting!

MARIE ANNE: So you and Wilf did not…

PATSY: Did not what?

MARIE ANNE: Uhm-uhm'd?

PATSY: No! Gosh No! Why in the world would you think that, Marie Anne?

MARIE ANNE: Puring said/

WILF: PURING?

Enter PURING.

PURING: Yes?

WILF stares at PURING. Turns and stares at PENNY. Then looks at PURING again.

WILF: P...p...p...

PURING: Puring.

WILF turns to look at PENNY.

WILF: P...p...p...

PENNY: Penny.

Beat. Beat. Beat.

PATSY: Oh. My. God. WILF! YOU CAN'T TELL THEM APART?!

DR. MILES and MARIE ANNE speak the next two lines at the same time.

DR. MILES: Propesterous!
MARIE ANNE: Ridiculous!

WILF: Um. Sure I can.

PATSY: Prove it.

WILF: What?

PATSY: Close your eyes, Wilf.

WILF: This is stupid, Patsy.

PATSY: Do it! *(He does.)* Describe what Penny looks like.

WILF: Patsy, she's standing right over there. *(Points at PURING.)*

PATSY: What does she look like?

WILF: She's Filipino.

CHARLIE: That's both of 'em, you log.

WILF: She has a long black hair, beautiful brown eyes and a cute little nose.

PATSY, DR. MILES and MARIE ANNE speak the next three lines at the same time.

PATSY: Puring. Puring. Puring.
DR. MILES: Poppet. Poppet. Poppet.
MARIE ANNE: Penny. Puring. Penny.

WILF: She wears funny little rubber boots.

PURING: Me.

WILF: And sometimes wears a pretty silk scarf…

PENNY: Me.

WILF: …And has come to two of my hockey games…

PURING: Me.

WILF: I bought her a mango.

PENNY: Me.

WILF: She gave me some dried mango.

PURING: Me.

WILF: And…she fainted. She fainted on the day they arrived. I held her in my arms and/

PATSY: And you stared into each other's eyes and it was love at first sight.

WILF: Penny?

PURING: *(Beat.)* Me.

WILF: What? No. Puring?

PATSY: And that's why when you kissed Penny, no fireworks! It all makes sense!

WILF: Puring? Not Penny?

PATSY: Yes.

WILF: *(To PURING.)* You?

PURING: Yes. Me.

WILF: And you're *not* engaged?

PURING: No.

WILF: I feel dizzy.

PURING: How could you think that I was…

PENNY: …that she is me?

DR. MILES: Really, Wilf. How could you?

MARIE ANNE: Shut it, Miles.

WILF: I…I…I don't know. I'm just…plain…stupid I guess.

(To PURING.) I wish you could have read my letter.

PURING: I did.

WILF: You did?

CHARLIE: You got no business writing letters or kissing anybody, Wilf. You're engaged.

PATSY/
DR. MILES/
MARIE ANNE/
PENNY/
PURING: You're engaged?!

WILF: I'm not! Not anymore. I called Donna yesterday and broke off the engagement. It was a long time coming. We'd been engaged since we were eighteen, but I've been away most of the time. And, well, it wasn't really working out and we just kinda fizzled out, you know. But I didn't have the guts to do anything about it, until, well, until the day that the nurses came. You, Puring, fainted and…well…umm…

PURING: I think I know what you are talking about.

MARIE ANNE: Will someone please explain it to me?!

PATSY: Wilf loves Puring. Love at first sight! Just like the movies.

MARIE ANNE: But what about you and Wilf?

PATSY: There is no me and Wilf. I'm with Hank!

PURING: You are?

PATSY: We are officially going steady!

MARIE ANNE: And Penny and Wilf?

PENNY: I am engaged. Romi is coming in two weeks.

MARIE ANNE: My head is spinning.

CHARLIE: Sit down, Marie Anne. Let me get you some coffee. I think we all could use a break.

DR. MILES: So you won't be needing my gun after all, Charlie.

CHARLIE: *(To PENNY.)* Do you still want to go to Saskatoon?

PENNY: Yes, Mr. Govenlock. I think it's best. I hope you understand, Mrs. Lussier.

MARIE ANNE: I think so, dear. I'm sorry for all the chaos. This has been quite the night. Why don't you turn in, and Charlie'll drive you in the morning? Right, Charlie?

CHARLIE: Sure thing. Let me take your bags.

PENNY: Thank you. Good night.

PENNY exits followed by CHARLIE.

MARIE ANNE: Come along, Miles. Let's finish the rounds.

DR. MILES: After you, Marie Anne.

MARIE ANNE: You too, Patsy.

PATSY: Aw, but, I just want to…I mean, maybe Wilf and Puring need me to…

MARIE ANNE: You've done enough helping for a lifetime, Patsy.

MARIE ANNE, PATSY and DR. MILES exit.

PURING: Wilf Klassen, you look hurt.

WILF: I've taken a lot of pucks to the face, but nothing hurt as much as Charlie's right hook.

PURING: Wilf Klassen…

WILF: Wilf, just Wilf, remember?

PURING: I've changed my mind.

WILF: About what?

PURING: My favorite Beatles song.

She smiles and offers WILF her hand. She helps him stand up. Still holding hands, they smooch. Fireworks.

The end.